# POETRY NOW NORTH
# & NORTH WEST
# ENGLAND 2004

Edited by

Heather Killingray

First published in Great Britain in 2004 by
*POETRY NOW*
Remus House,
Coltsfoot Drive,
Peterborough, PE2 9JX
Telephone (01733) 898101
Fax (01733) 313524

SB ISBN 1 84460 845 X

# *FOREWORD*

Although we are a nation of poets we are accused of not reading poetry, or buying poetry books. After many years of listening to the incessant gripes of poetry publishers, I can only assume that the books they publish, in general, are books that most people do not want to read.

Poetry should not be obscure, introverted, and as cryptic as a crossword puzzle: it is the poet's duty to reach out and embrace the world.

The world owes the poet nothing and we should not be expected to dig and delve into a rambling discourse searching for some inner meaning.

The reason we write poetry (and almost all of us do) is because we want to communicate: an ideal; an idea; or a specific feeling. Poetry is as essential in communication, as a letter; a radio; a telephone, and the main criterion for selecting the poems in this anthology is very simple: they communicate.

# CONTENTS

| | | |
|---|---|---|
| Beggar | Alex Anderson | 1 |
| Nostalgia | Edith Antrobus | 2 |
| Love Emit, Emit | Keith Conyers-Nolan | 3 |
| Music Of The Forest | Vanessa Staunton | 4 |
| My Angel's Lament | John Hill | 5 |
| Storm On The Mersey | Danielle Ward | 6 |
| A Liverpool Gem | Anna Gaskell | 7 |
| Half-Past Midnight | Sheryl Starr | 8 |
| Love Is . . . | Amanda Clarke | 9 |
| Early Bird | L Finlayson | 10 |
| Ode To Desert Orchid | Christine Skeer | 11 |
| Untitled | Amy Gilmore | 12 |
| We Met Once | S J Burton | 13 |
| Longing For Love | Christina Appleton | 14 |
| Joy Of Living? | Captain Valentine Daly | 15 |
| Memories Of Park Road, Dingle (1947) | Barbara Berry | 16 |
| Skies | Pauline Caton | 17 |
| Tiggy And Giz | Patricia Bradley | 18 |
| Evacuation September 1939 | B Haworth | 19 |
| My Brother Robert | Joyce Grounds | 20 |
| My Words | Peter Royston Cole | 22 |
| Found And Lost | Jane Corcoran | 23 |
| La Belle Vache | Patricia Hayes | 24 |
| Paradise | S A Almond | 25 |
| Gibraltar | Christine Rowley | 26 |
| Shipwreck | Rita Rogers | 28 |
| Daffodils | N Daly | 29 |
| New | Dave Hughes | 30 |
| Perils Of The Sea | Neil Bellew | 31 |
| A Sacrifice Of Motherhood | Esmond Simcock | 32 |
| My Slumbering Child | Carol May | 34 |
| Calm Seas Of Time | Lee Tellis Adams | 35 |
| Writing In Verse Is A Curse | Jacqui Dunne | 36 |
| Friday Shopping | Pat Ammundsen | 37 |
| Passing Neighbours | Hannah Fleming | 38 |

| | | |
|---|---|---|
| Autumn Gold | Patricia Johnson | 39 |
| Thank You | Rebecca Guest | 40 |
| Recycle | Gwen Gibson | 41 |
| Lovely Carer | Sandra Jebb | 42 |
| It's Our Turn To Give | | |
| A Presentation | Andy Jones | 43 |
| Maria | Joan P Godfrey | 44 |
| Scotland | Joan Harris | 45 |
| Me | J A Carter | 46 |
| Emotions | M Lyon | 47 |
| Air Raid (Circa 1941) | G R Bell | 48 |
| Anniversary 2000 | M C Jones | 49 |
| The Sun, Moon And Stars | Emma Sweeney | 50 |
| Forgiven | Andrew John Stevenson | 51 |
| For The Love Of Oliver | | |
| - Our Cocker Spaniel | Carole Umpleby | 52 |
| My Son Mark | Pat Seddon | 53 |
| Tomorrow | Angela Dolphin | 54 |
| Come Hear My Cry | Kevin Eccleston | 55 |
| After | Dawn L Edwards | 56 |
| A Man's Best Friend | Charles Henry | 57 |
| The Colours Of The Rainbow | April Dickinson-Owen | 58 |
| Disco Dancer | D J Totten | 59 |
| Cumbria | Robbie Ellis | 60 |
| Self | A Sheard | 62 |
| Spring | Beryl Barlow | 63 |
| Liverpool | Alison Tichy | 64 |
| What Am I? | Nicola Preston | 65 |
| Solway | John Rowland Parker | 66 |
| Keld Chapel | Katie Hale | 67 |
| Forever England | Jan Courtenay | 68 |
| Nature Boy | Brian O'Brien | 69 |
| The Shadow | Marie Ryder | 70 |
| Boca Chica: | Gillian Ripley | 71 |
| Emotions Of The Indian Ocean | Michael Cunningham | 72 |
| Memories | Patricia Hampson Curry | 73 |
| Appreciate Your Senses | J Grooby | 74 |
| The Child Sweepers | Peter Owen | 75 |

| | | |
|---|---|---|
| Easter Time | Norah Rawlinson | 76 |
| Snowdrops | Deborah Storey | 77 |
| Cool And Clear | Carol John | 78 |
| Firefighters Of The Blitz | Neil Kelly | 79 |
| Sunset | Linda J Liggett | 80 |
| His Gifts | ABC | 81 |
| The Elephants | Eileen Todd | 82 |
| Turbine Turmoil | D T Pendit | 83 |
| Time | Tony Turner | 84 |
| From The Heart | Joan Thompson | 85 |
| Lost Love | Amanda Weir | 86 |
| Knock Back | Isaac Smart | 87 |
| A Time In Summer | Bethan Williams | 88 |
| Senses Awakening | Louise Jones | 89 |
| Little Raindrop | Martin James Banasko | 90 |
| I Hate Fishing | Chris Thomas | 91 |
| Happy Times | Joanne Basnett | 92 |
| Untitled | Thomas Conor | 93 |
| Liverpool | Edna Sarsfield | 94 |
| Old Age | W Atherton | 95 |
| House Clearance | Gina Riley | 96 |
| My Teacher | Kelly Gibbons | 97 |
| Panic Attack | James Kitts | 98 |
| Friends Are Like Angels | Vicky Tam | 99 |
| Could I Be Wrong | James Ayrey | 100 |
| The Meaning Of Life | Joanne Cross | 101 |
| You | Carlene Montoute | 102 |
| A Mortal Blow | Katy Flynn | 103 |
| High And Above | Irene Clare Garner | 104 |
| Time | Stacie-Nicolle Mortimer | 105 |
| Fish In The Sea | Umar Azam | 106 |
| The Runaway | Carole J Fury | 107 |
| Premonition | Laura Howarth-Kirke | 108 |
| Joy | Paul Shipley | 110 |
| Earth | Lynsey Gill | 112 |
| Ring | Joy Ottey | 114 |
| Sainthood | Adhel Azad | 115 |

Manchester 3000:

| | | |
|---|---|---|
| Planning Report | Elizabeth Parish | 116 |
| Saint Peter's Square, Manchester | Edith Ward | 117 |
| The Man Sitting Under The Tree | Rachel Van Den Bergen | 118 |
| Roller Coaster | K Baskin | 119 |
| The Remnants Of War | Dellis Barracks | 120 |
| For A Friend | Peter James Cox | 122 |
| My Stars | Colin Horn | 123 |
| Reminiscence | Adrian Salamon | 124 |
| Thank You | Lisa Killeen | 125 |
| The Hour | C M Creedon | 126 |
| Music To The Ears | L E Marchment | 127 |
| God Is My Strength | Ann Margaret Rowell | 128 |
| Laughter | Jim Rogerson | 129 |
| Better Times | C E Kelly | 130 |
| The Dusty Cry | May Forcman | 131 |
| Gun | M Sheikh | 132 |
| Though Of Bowland | Tim Hoare | 134 |
| Desire | Paul Kelly | 135 |
| Evil Dread | Raven | 136 |
| Immune | Andrew Gibson | 137 |
| A Prayer For Bruce Wayne | Robert B Appleton | 138 |
| The Appeal | Debbie Morgan | 139 |
| My Melancholy Wish | Keith Tissington | 140 |
| Never Will I Leave You | Ray Varley | 141 |
| For The Love Of Our Planet | Lyn Wilkinson | 142 |
| The Poet's Dawn | Trevor De Luca | 143 |
| Untitled | Tracey Dixon | 144 |
| Me | Janette Dann | 145 |
| The Dance Around The Sun | A F Mace | 146 |
| Lost In Time And Space | Brian M Wood | 147 |
| And So The Wheel Turns | Simon Martin | 148 |
| Death Has No Memory | Christopher M David | 149 |
| Dad | Tash | 150 |
| He Is Not Dead, But Sleeping | Jane Hinchcliff | 151 |
| Hot Summer Night | Elizabeth M Rait | 152 |
| The Lonely Demon | Wesley James Byrne | 153 |
| Tender Love, Sweet Kisses | Donald John Tye | 154 |

| | | |
|---|---|---|
| Songbird | Teresa Kelly | 155 |
| Where Is The Child? | Carole A M Johnson | 156 |
| Talent From Birth | Joyce Hemsley | 157 |
| A Day Out In Whitby | Elizabeth Marsay | 158 |
| Irene | Catherine M Simpson | 159 |
| World War Two | Laura Thompson | 160 |
| What I Saw | Lizzie Cooper | 161 |
| Sitwell Stein I Wish | Pauline Smithson | 162 |
| Lilla Cross | M Urquhart | 164 |
| Ancient And Modern | Alan Whitworth | 165 |
| Silent Battle | Beth Lomas | 166 |
| Lady In Waiting | Lesley Ann Ball | 167 |
| Drifting | Angela Pritchard | 168 |
| World Of Cheese | Caroline Crowther | 170 |
| 500 Miles | Paul Bracken | 171 |
| Keys | Colin Williamson | 172 |
| Morning Walk To Whitby | Gillian Orton | 173 |
| Seasons | Kimberley Jenkinson | 174 |
| Forgotten Land | John Mutton | 175 |
| One Night In Pennywell | Julie Long | 176 |
| Far Beyond Fey Weatherheath | Alexander David Graham | 177 |
| The New Pit Baths | Alex Branthwaite | 178 |
| Life's Cycle | Kathleen Potter | 179 |
| Dear Friend | Mary Veronica Ciarella Murray | 180 |
| Valentine's Day | Alan C Brown | 181 |
| Flowers In Spring | Adrian Brett | 182 |
| Meant To Be | John Robinson | 183 |
| Immobile | George Carrick | 184 |
| Picnic Checklist | Marie A Golan | 185 |
| Down At Quarry Bank Mill | Nikky Braithwaite | 186 |
| My Manchester | Margaret Doherty | 187 |
| Contemporary Fossils | Lee Simpson | 188 |
| Looking | P Allinson | 189 |
| The Green Room | Sara Newby | 190 |
| It's Funny How | Jessica Copland | 191 |
| The Listener | Rachel Lucinda Burns | 192 |
| My Cat | Jennie Stott | 193 |
| Habbaniya Shadows | Elsie Scrowther | 194 |

| | | |
|---|---|---|
| She Is Here | June Macfarlane | 195 |
| Bitter Silence | Claire Cockburn | 196 |
| In Love And Proud | Victoria A Miller | 197 |
| Military Misery | Frank Littlewood | 198 |
| Road Of Friendship | Jacqueline Bolt | 199 |
| Awake | Rajiv Sankaranarayanan | 200 |
| My Secret Place | Dave Sim | 201 |
| Cirencester Abbey | Ann Heath | 202 |
| Anger | Angela C Oldroyd | 203 |
| To Mum | Janet Cavill | 204 |
| A Spring Poem | M Cook | 205 |
| My Wavertree | Jack Gray | 206 |
| Snapshot | Sheila Anderson | 207 |
| The Essence Of Nature | Andrew Gruberski | 208 |
| Respect | Lorna Lea | 209 |
| Holderness Spring | Graham Wade | 210 |
| Time | Margaret Dennison | 211 |
| Spring | Roy Hare | 212 |
| Colour Of Water | J Millington | 213 |
| Lavender Bushes | Anne Hamlett | 214 |
| Fish Tour | Howard Peach | 215 |
| Black Gold | Carol Kaye | 216 |
| My City And I | Bruce Barnes | 217 |
| A Village Pond | David Bielby | 218 |
| Untouched | Matthew Wilson | 219 |
| The Word Of God | Leslie Bailey | 220 |
| Chaos | Nadia Hashim | 221 |
| In Passing | Victoria Bonner | 222 |
| Cold Turkey | Maddoc Martin | 223 |
| On Swirl How | Ken Parker | 224 |
| Visiting My Aunt | P Jennison | 225 |
| Spoils Of War | E M Doyle | 226 |
| Ladies Of A Certain Age | Delyse Holmes | 227 |
| Our Mother Earth | Gordon Greenfield | 228 |
| True Love Truth | Ian Godfrey | 229 |
| What Have You Done For Me? | Parveen Saini | 230 |
| The Hospital Visit | Laura Chaplin | 231 |
| The Summer Rose | Shirley May Croxford | 232 |

| | | |
|---|---|---|
| Mermaid | Brenda Artingstall | 233 |
| Ode To Charlie B | Stephen J Bolton | 234 |
| Bridlington Heroes | Mike Wilson | 236 |
| Bradford (West Yorkshire) | Coleen Bradshaw | 237 |
| First Meeting | Rebecca Culpan | 238 |
| The Ferryboat | Muriel Mabon | 240 |
| Music Man | Dan Maughan | 241 |
| What Is Mine Is Yours | Renate Fekete | 242 |
| It's Only Money | Susie Field | 243 |

## BEGGAR

Turning over in my mind
the meaning of our differences,
of partings, and of worlds
that make no sense,
I soothe all with a gesture.

(a world of mirrors
bearing no reflections)

And find that I have lifted
from your outstretched hand
a purse of loosened dogmas;
futile coinage for a dead belief.

*Alex Anderson*

# NOSTALGIA

I have a pleasant memory, just before the war,
Of a very cosy youth hostel in Wales.
All young people in love with life,
Exchanging some interesting tales.
The weather was hot, the sea was calm,
A very nice night for a dip.
All nationalities gathered together,
Making the most of the trip.
I met a charming boy called Anton,
He belonged to the Hitler Youth.
He said, 'Heil Hitler,' with the Nazi salute,
Which I thought was a little uncouth.
But he was so very polite and friendly,
He didn't look much like a foe,
Little did we think, that in a short time,
All these simple pleasures would go.
We were told there wouldn't be a war,
There would be a period of peace,
We never expected in the next year,
Our idyllic life would soon cease.
The cream of the country were pilots,
Young men just starting a new life,
Little knowing when they began training,
They would be starting the struggle and strife.
My young man joined up in the navy,
We decided to soon tie the knot,
So on a forty-eight hours leave we got married,
And made the most of the time we had got.
The Battle of Britain just looming ahead,
Would find some of these valiant airmen dead!

*Edith Antrobus*

## LOVE EMIT, EMIT

There's a slow, steady drip, drip
A filtered life trip, trip
A joy, purity, a right, skip, skip
That brings us to we

There's a common goal, aim, aim
A heartbeat the same, same
Always together again, again
That binds, we agree

There's a musical echo, drop, drop
A beautiful cut, crop, crop
A song, a tune, never stop, stop
That leads you to me

There's a glance, look, look
A kiss stolen, took, took
A world shaken, shook, shook
That helps you to feel

There's a finger snap, click, click
A tuneful tip, trick, trick
A type, a style, slick, slick
That sends I to thee

There's a look, glance, glance
A first hunt, chance, chance
Overcoming distance, new romance
That makes us both see

There's a thump, beat, beat
An internal rhythm, heat, heat
A promise, a gift, treat, treat
That prompts me to be.

*Keith Conyers-Nolan*

## MUSIC OF THE FOREST

Oh green, green glen I am here again, oh green, green glade,
You are fairy made, oh fragrant woodland shade,
Sweet and gentle wood, where everything is good,
Show me woodland creatures, send news from flower to tree,
Come gentle deer amidst the bluebells,
Turn your mellow gaze to me,
The green man plays a piping tune,
To float around me soon,
A melodic drifting sound, a fairy ring to go around
And gentle spirits come to dance
And I shall wait my chance, in a merry trance,
Come dance and sing, in the toadstool ring,
Songs of love, in harmony with the woodland birds,
Singing stories without words,
Echo a gentle note, that nobody wrote,
To sway the forest firs,
The tinkle of the waterfall,
The whispering oak so tall,
Here, where the red fox, need run no more,
There is peace in the forest and love is the law,
Fairy folk are dancing, they play their magic flutes,
Soon they feed on forest fruits,
Dreamy symphony, fairy melody, fluttering butterfly wings,
To sweet music of the forest, I shall dance and sing,
Among the elms, firs and birches and the blossoming tree,
This is where I wish to be,
Sweet music of the forest stay with me forever,
For, this is surely Heaven and I am surely free.

*Vanessa Staunton*

# MY ANGEL'S LAMENT

I'll always remember that night
An angel lay next to me bathed in the moonlight.
Despite my joy at her presence a thick silence hung in the air
My heart hung heavy as I lay stroking her hair.
I begged her to tell me her story that night
I wanted to comfort her, make everything all right.
Wiping away a tear my angel began
To lament her story to this little boy/man.
I was awe-struck at her boldness
Unselfishly bearing the world on her shoulders
She said her feathers were no longer bright
And I watched as her tears glistened in the moonlight
I blathered and stupid words spout
Try as I did, she still lay in doubt
So I held her close
*Actions speak so much louder than words*
With my arms around her she drifted to sleep
While around us the night softly creeped
I lay there awake watching her dream
While trying to remember the way her eyes used to gleam.
I lay here now in the absence of light
Alone with my memories and thoughts from that night
I think of my angel and where she might be
I wish she was here curled up next to me.
I want to clean the dirt from her wings
I want to help her face up to the bad things
But most of all I want to find the strength and boldness
So I can take the world's weight from her shoulders.

*John Hill*

## STORM ON THE MERSEY

The cloak of night silently draws in
And envelops the sleeping city of Liverpool.
The clouds work up a rage,
Wondrous purples and blacks swirling,
As the Liver building on the famous skyline,
Reach out to embrace them like old friends.
The wind skims the river teasingly,
Which is winding like a silver ribbon,
Heading out for sea.
Then, the wind becomes a howling, screeching monster,
Turning over anything in its way.
Lightning etches shards of light in the sky.
The clouds start crying
And huge tears splash into the tossing waves,
Which have travelled from the corners of the world.
The seabirds laugh at the tumbling waves,
As they play with a boat,
Like a cat with a mouse.

There's a show for Liverpool tonight,
There's a storm on the Mersey!

*Danielle Ward  (12)*

# A LIVERPOOL GEM

In springtime there is a special place
In Liverpool you must see
Fields of hope, fields of dreams
A yellow, dancing sea.

Babbling brooks with stepping stones
And a magical fairy glen
It's really worth checking out,
Even if you don't believe in them.

A crystal palace full of trees
With lots of tropical plants and leaves,
You may sit and relax all day,
For there is no charge for this array.

With sloping hills and boating lake,
A place of beauty, make no mistake
Go there now, you have been told
Just let Sefton Park unfold.

*Anna Gaskell  (12)*

# HALF-PAST MIDNIGHT

Half-past a dream
Just like a wish gone,
I see flashes before me
Like a tuneless, repetitive song.

Half-past my life
Like a caged bird of paradise,
Luxuries all guaranteed
But without love - nothing is nice.

Half-past midnight
Half-past my pain:
Both halves unreconciled
Like burning drops of summer rain.

*Sheryl Starr*

## LOVE IS . . .

Love . . . is so special, one of a kind
To not love you, I would lose my mind
The silly things that you say and do
Remind me every day just why I love you
I see your smile, you light my day
Because you are so wonderful
In every single way
Love is togetherness till death do us part
I will cherish and hold you forever in my heart
There have been times when it's not all bliss
But it's all worthwhile when we make up and kiss
We don't need the roses or the chocolate box
Because with our love combined
We are as solid as a rock.

*Amanda Clarke*

## EARLY BIRD

Early bird roams through the cold kitchen
Of a house which still perspires the silent
Sweat of sleep. Fearful of the first noise
You must make; the clattering of spoons
And forks on the tabletop, the rushing of the
Water in the pipes, the slamming of a door.
Eyes go sore at yesterday's mess, the
Dirty towels and puddles on the floor.

A sea mist hangs outside the window
And spring's slow jog has speeded up
To a canter. Early bird can hear the hooves
Clip-clopping behind the ticking of the clock.

A robin redbreast perches - like a mystery
On the bare finger of a branch pointing
Into the dripping mist.

*L Finlayson*

## ODE TO DESERT ORCHID

*(From one of his many racing fans)*

Desert Orchid's one hell of a horse
With that we all agree
The finest at any racecourse
The punters could wish to see

His spectacular leaps are enthralling
Of his courage there is no doubt
We don't want to think of him falling
We just want to cheer and shout

He loves the track at Kempton
The King George is his feat
He's even conquered Cheltenham
There's nothing left to beat

From two miles up to three miles plus
The distance matters not
He does it all without a fuss
And gives it all he's got

He knows when racing to the post
His nose must pass it first
And this is when he tries the most
To find a final burst

Let's hope there's lots more races
For Dessie to contest
To bring smiles to our faces
And to prove he is the best

To owner Richard Burridge
Our thanks are here to stay
For giving us Desert Orchid
The wonderful flying grey.

*Christine Skeer*

# UNTITLED

When the world is finally silent,
when our voices are no longer heard.
When for a moment no one is speaking,
there's not even the song of a bird.

As we all share a minute of silence,
as we all stand together as one.
Without a thought we just listen,
as all our problems are gone.

Then we will thankfully see,
that the world is a beautiful place.
Without a single word said,
just miles of silence and space.

*Amy Gilmore  (13)*

## WE MET ONCE

We met once
Down a long
Park road
Amidst a scene
Of winter snow
A long time ago

You shook your head
I waved a fist
We silently passed
A sad lament that led the way
Would last eternally

I saw you again
By the old bandstand
I waved long
But the rain came
Down and drowned
Your hopes

And once more at
The cottage bar
You visited me
As you had done before
A bitter-sweet song
Of pain

We met again 5 years on
The same long road
The same sad song
The sad lament
That leads the way
Down the road
Of eternity.

*S J Burton*

## LONGING FOR LOVE

I'm sat here behind these bars, longing for you to come.
I'm willing to forgive what my past owners have done.
Ignore my broken body and look into my eyes,
For my love is unconditional and will never die.
My head is sore but I want to nuzzle it in your lap,
My paw is broken but I want you to stroke it whilst I nap,
My tongue is cut but I want to lick you with love,
My legs are hurting but I'd still love to fetch you your glove.
I would love to be your best friend and give you all my affection;
I would love to be by your side forever and give you my protection.
I'll be here to greet you when you're homeward bound
And promise to be good company for you as long as I'm around.
My body may be broken but my soul still shines bright
And I may now be blind in one eye but I'll never leave your sight.
Please take me home and give me your loving care
Because how much I want to love you is more than I can bear.

*Christina Appleton*

# JOY OF LIVING?

To sing a song when wine flows free
Or dance when tune pipes merrily?
To play at games with fine endeavour
Or stride o'er hills of gorse and heather?

To lie with poets and learned sages,
Or gaze on treasures of the ages?
To see the wonders of the world
And have life's beauty thus unfurled?

To fly a plane: to sail a boat
Or ride a horse in scarlet coat?
To fire a shot at beast of prey,
Or lead the van unto the fray?

I crave not one of these above,
Happiness is mine alone through love,
Love to each other forever giving
Brings to me the joy of living.

To hold your hand: to see you smile,
To touch your hair is more worthwhile
To share with you your joys and sorrows,
Today and through all life's tomorrows.

***Captain Valentine Daly***

# MEMORIES OF PARK ROAD, DINGLE (1947)

There's a road in Dingle everyone knows
With its shops and pubs where everyone goes
Eric's for chips, Prescot's for meat
The Gaumont for pictures where you queued for a seat.

The Sally Army was there for you to be saved
The ancient chapel was opposite where gravestones were paved.
There were doctors and dentists, an optician as well
And Ivor Jones' chemist with medicines to sell.

Ray's for your cups and a bank for your money
The Maypole and Co-op for groceries and honey
Laws for your paraffin and your soap too
Anna's for gowns made specially for you.

The Coach and Horses where we drank and we sang
And always got merry with a pint in our hand.
Also the pub with Jessie Appleton's name
Where you could play darts or have a domino game.

Lavels was the herb shop with seats on poles
And also wood seats with punched out holes
Over the hill was Sturlas check shop
And Charlotte's the place where your life came to a stop.

*Barbara Berry*

## SKIES

Let your skies be forever blue.
May hope and peace see you through.
As clouds pass gently by,
You look into the heavens and wonder why?

Why are the skies so blue some days?
And why sometimes oh so grey?
When your heart is full of joy and love
Your skies are beautiful above.

When your soul is full of sorrow
And things seem as though there's no tomorrow.
Just remember that behind the clouds the sun is shining,
Your grey skies have a silver lining.

Grey skies do not last forever
And blue skies replace the sullen weather.
Live in hope and sweet content,
Bring joy and happiness, in time well spent.

*Pauline Caton*

## TIGGY AND GIZ
*(Dedicated to 'Greyhounds R Us')*

Your owners couldn't keep you, what was your fate to be?
Together you might find a home, or maybe separately.
Peter typed your story; put you on the site,
Both of you together, what a saddened plight.
No one wants two greyhounds; they say we are too old,
Can no one open up their hearts and consider us two sold?
Well, maybe not this time, it wasn't meant to be
We'll wait and maybe next time, we'll be happy, homed and free.

*Patricia Bradley*

## EVACUATION SEPTEMBER 1939

Thinking back upon those years,
as 'vaccy-ees' we had no fears
about the future and the past
- nor even stopped to think how fast
the years would fly -
or wonder why.
We took for granted every minute
now, we're just glad that
we're still in it!

*B Haworth*

## MY BROTHER ROBERT

My brother Robert
Would be forty-seven
But he is not here
He is up in Heaven

My brother Robert
Was placed in a bowl
Naked and tiny
Losing his soul

My mother Margaret
Got out of bed
Washed him
And dressed him
And then she said

'Robert is sleeping
He will soon be awake
Please don't disturb him
My son you can't take.'

My father then entered
With tears on his face
And into his strong arms
Robert was placed

'A walk in the park,'
That's what he said
He couldn't tell Margaret
Her newborn was dead

Tiny white casket
He carried alone
His heart about broken
As they both left home

Robert my brother
Laid gently to rest
For mother and father
The hardest test

I never knew him
I was born later on
'A miracle baby'
For whom the sun shone

But in our memories
Now we are three
Lives my brother Robert
Who was born before me.

*Joyce Grounds*

## MY WORDS

If I could write my words with leaves
that fall from trees
in autumn,
what a bonfire would come soon.

If I could write my words with sand
I know it would be found
that all this land
would instantly become a dune.

If I could write my words with water
I would surely drown,
from the messages I would put down.

Love you now and always.

*Peter Royston Cole*

## FOUND AND LOST

By the warm blue sea
She brought a cold north wind to wake him.
With a white-hot poker to his heart
her eyes told him that she knew
he'd slept years and now would never rest again.
His love from a lifetime past,
he remembered their tearing apart.
But she was only passing
And it was not to be,
How he ached to hold her
and burn her image on his soul.
The connection was made
And she was gone,
His home, his home, his one.

*Jane Corcoran*

## LA BELLE VACHE

You may think it strange somehow,
That I adore the humble cow
It walks the fields with gentle grace
And has a truly lovely face.

I like all cows - whatever breed
But if I ever felt the need
To choose a favourite
It would be the black-eyed cow of Normandy.

Herefords, Jerseys, Charolet
No doubt there is a lot to say
For all these lovely bovine creatures
But when it comes to perfect features
None can beat the black-ringed eyes
That gaze at you in mild surprise
From underneath an apple tree
In early spring - in Normandy.

*Patricia Hayes*

## PARADISE

Sky-blue ocean laps onto
the harvest-golden sands,
palm trees of tropical green shade me
from the sunbeam,
rays beat down onto
this lazy land.

This is the life for me laughing and resting
near the sea,
feeling its occasional mint
cool breeze.

The waves do not crash they just
happily sail forth and back.
With such tranquil beauty by my side,
I have no doubts,
that I am in paradise.

*S A Almond*

# GIBRALTAR

The rock has seen the beginning and the end,
Steadfast, guarding, protective friend,
But in that November I could not see,
I only saw dolphins wild and free,
Foaming waves forever churning,
Unpredictable, wild and yearning,
Looking to Africa, across the strait,
Not knowing that soon a new love would await,
Thrilling my senses with his romance,
A wild adventure, breathtaking dance,
Devotion and passion, hopes and dreams,
Words on the Net, plans and schemes
Longing and hoping, I love you forever
Imagining the time we would spend together.
I enjoyed the feelings of not being alone,
Bringing sunshine to my lifeless home.
My spirit awakened, my soul alive,
Against all odds we would survive,
I fought for you, struggled for you, on and on,
For jobs and a visa when it seemed hope was gone,
I honoured my promises and clung to my dreams,
But in the back of my mind things were not as they seemed,
You know, you were always a mystery to me,
Not on the Net when you were meant to be,
My doubts and fears growing until the days,
Like sandcastles disappearing into the waves,
It made me sad as I heard less from you,
Don't leave me please, tell me what's true,
Like a snake you slithered, weaving one lie to the next,
Then no word from you, not even a text,
It took a stranger to tell me what was really true,
It was a lie from the start, now I have no respect for you,
All you brought me was grief and pain,
Turmoil and upset, greed and lies again.

Now two years on near the rock, on the rolling sea,
There are no dolphins today, just cold bravery,
An accept of hurt, of sorrow and pain,
Of trying your utmost to no mortal gain,
Like a sailor's spirit, not subdued, always there,
Rain starts to fall, but the wind's still in my hair,
And as long as the wild wind spirits on,
When others would be crushed and all hope gone,
I know I will survive.

*Christine Rowley*

## SHIPWRECK

I was a ship, I sailed the waves
and fought a thousand gales.
My mast so high it touched
the sky.

But, in the fog I got lost,
I still fought against the waves but,
I grew weaker in the midst
of my daze.

My bow broke and I almost choked,
I tried not to sink but,
I couldn't think.

When daylight came I couldn't believe that
was me,
I was shipwrecked and downtrodden.

*Rita Rogers*

# DAFFODILS

During spring she can't understand him
for months daffodils are his world.
She despises each brazen flower from
petal to stem, the way she has hated
every woman that has ever come between them.

During spring daffodils are his world.
When he retired as headman at the park
she had hoped he might give up his passion
for spills of golden heads, freshly unfurled.

During spring she can barely get a word out of him
she used to laugh at him because he guarded each specimen
like a semi-precious stone or a pearl.
That was until she heard that he named
each bud after dancing girls
he met when he played the trumpet in a jazz band.

During spring she grows tired of his vigil.
He insists on sleeping and eating daffodils in the shed.
Whilst she fantasises about chopping off their heads.

*N Daly*

## NEW

Spring is here, uncoiling
Time for some pleasant toiling

Gardens now starting to glow
Colour is truly on the go

Trees are standing to attention
After months of no mention

Kittens playing on the grass
No longer a frightening morass

Watch the changes every hour
Smell the fragrance of every flower

And after summer, don't shed a tear
Spring will be back again, next year.

*Dave Hughes*

# PERILS OF THE SEA

On a cold April night
Many crew and passengers
Did not know what was in sight

For a large iceberg was dead ahead
Two-and-a-half hours' time, many will be dead

When the iceberg hit the ship
RMS Titanic would start to dip

When the final lifeboat was finally clear
Many cried with fear
For everyone knew by then
The end was near
To call that ship unsinkable
Sadly was a fatal mistake.

Due to the fact 1,500 lives
Of men, women, children,
The sea did take.

*Neil Bellew*

# A SACRIFICE OF MOTHERHOOD

This is a very special day
For mothers everywhere
It's more than just a bunch of flowers
There's love and joy and care

A mother is eternal
Introduced when time began
God knew what He was doing
When He created man

Arriving on our planet
A help-meet to become
A very special person
We just call her Mum

It's a mother who comes running
When her child has slipped and fell
She rubs the bruise and grazes
Then bends to kiss them well

She's the greatest story teller
That the world has ever know
And no one knows the times she weeps
When sitting all alone

When sons are slain in battle
It's for their mums they call
If sickness ravages their frame
She will sacrifice her all

One mother even saw her son
Bruised, whipped and crucified
If only she could have the choice
For him she would have died

You're wished a happy Mother's Day
From your girl or perhaps your boy
Life would be grim without you
With love from your bundle of joy.

*Esmond Simcock*

## My Slumbering Child

You sleep, with hand outstretched
and unknowingly caress my face.
I gaze in awe at your perfection.

Your brow unlined by youth,
your mouth so soft and innocent.
The miracle of nature.

Your skin shines with a dewy freshness,
unwilted by life's caress.
Vulnerable and trusting. My precious child.

I marvel, as you are guided
to that place of dreams -
a tranquillity that childhood affords.

The peace you exude is almost tenable,
a contentment only a child could impart.
Slumbering serenely, sinless and chaste.

The breath of life you exhale
is but the purest, matched only by
the gold mass that envelops your pillow.

This flawless picture of innocence
is but to be marvelled at and consumed.
For life itself offers no purer picture.

*Carol May*

# CALM SEAS OF TIME

The stars in the ocean flicker and burn
Imprisoned by time and the sunlight's return
The moon in the lake echoes alone
Throughout the woodlands ripples its moan.

The howl and the whisper blinded by age
The darkness envelops you in your shadow's rage
The herald of dawn, all that remains for the lost
The night mime he listens, he reigns through the lost.

He wraps them in nothingness and thrives on their fear
Feeds on the tense air and drinks from a tear
Death before life, night after night
Sleeps as a carcass that burns in the light.

He can't see his prison nor feel his strings
The silence grows thicker as he so-called sings
The lost see him as a god, the one with a path
He knows of no direction or why he's under this wrath.

Lonely is the wolf among a flock of sheep
Stealing another midnight in hope of a memory to keep
Soulless are the mime and wolf, brothers of the night
Their enemy the darkness
And more so is the light.

*Lee Tellis Adams*

## WRITING IN VERSE IS A CURSE

I'd love to write a poem
That simply didn't rhyme
I'd love to be like old Ted Hughes
And have a mismatched line

I long to write in modern prose
Contemporary, smart verse
But when I try, it always rhymes
It's monstrous, it's a curse!

I'm sitting now, my pen all hot
From jotting down these lines
But yet again
To my dismay
The wretched thing's in rhyme

I'm all fatigued
I'm all worn out
My efforts are in vain
No matter what I seem to write
I always end . . . in a similar manner
*(Success!)*

*Jacqui Dunne*

## FRIDAY SHOPPING

Six bottles of wine, large bar of chocolate
Packet of chewing gum to freshen breath
Smart body spray, the best
Nicotine patches to help fend off death.

All this in his basket as he waits in the queue
I muse on the load and guess,
So, he's giving up smoking and impressing his bird
Not young, but smart in his dress.

Through the till and he pauses, the cashier awaits
Voucher produced for the wine.
'So sorry sir, I cannot accept, no card, no discount.'
All his plans dashed on the line.

Fuse short he explodes, 'Oh keep it,' he snarls
And flees from the till minus basket.
Sneaks back to reclaim the nicotine patches,
Poor fellow he's just blown his gasket.

*Pat Ammundsen*

# PASSING NEIGHBOURS

Is that who built a robot
Or that the man who cried,
'No,'
That's the one with the handsome
Son
He said the man had died

That's who looked after those children
Without a mum
And stayed with them
Till the day was done

It's I who wore a red suit
To the funeral
And I who said a prayer
Which made their hearts full.

***Hannah Fleming***

## AUTUMN GOLD

Shadows are longer, it's a shorter day
The sun is fading its weaker rays
There's a chill in the air
My favourite time of the year
The garden's still in bloom
Flowers still emitting their perfume
The cool breeze scatters petals that fall to the ground
Bees gather the last of the pollen they have found
While trees rustle their leaves
Very soon they will scatter and fall
Golden, russet and red to carpet the lawn
My feathered friends they shelter in their favourite shrub
Fluttering, flitting, swooping for scattered seed or grub
They collect the leaves or twigs to build a cosy nest
To shelter from the autumn chill and winter's cruel jest
Till springtime comes around again
A warming, welcome guest.

*Patricia Johnson*

## THANK YOU

For that little act of kindness that you did,
for those kind little words that you spoke.
For the care that shines through your loving eyes,
for when you give me a glimmer of hope.

When you show love through being who you are,
when your humanity is allowed to be.
When you embrace me in your arms with warmth,
when you thank me for being me.

I want to say thank you for loving who I am,
I want to say thank you for your care.
I want to hold you in my arms so tight,
I want to open up with you and share.

For feeling thanks within myself
is a wonderful feeling to embrace.
For I cherish to look and see your love
that's reflected in your smiling face.

*Rebecca Guest*

## RECYCLE

Recycle, recycle, it is our duty
    To make this world a place of beauty
Every day we must work very hard
    Save all your paper, envelopes and card
Carry your plastics to the recycle bin
    Glass as well, it can all go in
Your tins, cans and cartons can all be saved
    Teach the children this is the way to behave
Carrier bags - they won't rot down
    Take them back to the supermarket in town
Litter we can all pick up to be sure
    It's really not so much of a chore
Enter the spirit, protect the Earth
    Respect our planet - it's not such hard work!

*Gwen Gibson*

## LOVELY CARER

My husband has an illness, I don't know what to do
Sometimes I don't feel all that bad, sometimes I feel so blue
There's nothing I can do or say, to take the pain away
Except to hope and pray that soon will come a better day
We try to make the best of things, but sometimes it's so hard
We wonder why sometimes in life you're dealt a nasty card
We have our ups, we have our downs, just like most people do
But no one really understands just what we both go through
I try to make him better, but can only do so much
Sometimes it takes it out of him, all I can do is watch
And so I try to make him smile in oh so many ways
But then there's times when nothing helps, God do I hate those days
I sometimes sit and wonder, I sit and think a lot
About this cruel illness, this illness that we've got
Although he's got this illness I'll see it to the end
Cos after all is said and done, he's still my greatest friend
I must be feeling sad today, to write my feelings down
Tomorrow might be happier and maybe I won't frown
But as things go we'll wait and see just what tomorrow brings
And hope that when we wake again, we'll hear the spring birds sing
I think I'm feeling better now, I've got it off my chest
I think I'll go and have a nap, I do deserve the rest.

*Sandra Jebb*

## IT'S OUR TURN TO GIVE A PRESENTATION

Let's go to the bar and drink.
It might help us to think.
We've had a talk,
We've had a walk,
Now it's our turn to pick up the chalk.

*Andy Jones*

## MARIA

I am Maria, named after Ave Maria,
An elderly Spanish peasant lady.
My ancient home is the theatre of my whole existence.
As a child learning that important catechism from my parents,
Those questions and answers that help to unravel the journey of life,
Learning to understand the different moods of nature,
Working in the fields,
Taking a laden donkey to market,
Drawing strength from my church and its religion,
Graduating to marriage and family and their independence.

I thank God for my life
And now the theatre is a cinema of memories that sustain me.
Do not be misled by my wizened face,
For the will is as strong as ever,
The mind keen,
The memories so sharp
    As if they are projecting every day onto a screen.

*Joan P Godfrey*

## SCOTLAND

Forever beautiful in its skies
And rides the hill like crested birds
In mulls and vales and tracted eyes
Which feast upon its every word.
In cultured ways of youth and glow
Which curtailed honour of the clan
And plaided soldiers bagpipes blow
To rich enforce in tuneful plan.
But like the pipes of Pan they sing
And like the dew that fills each heart
And like the voices laughter rings
In consolation as they start.
To tread their way across each glen
And keep the hour from which did fall
The ways and wants of Scotland's men
Who answered each and every call.
O'ch I would wander hand in hand
And serve my life in valleys cool
Yes, I would ponder in that land
That gives its all to friend and fool.
But Scotland, land of lochs and hills
And bonnie lasses in the dells
And deepest voices in the choir
Send out their song in sounding bells.
Oft have I wandered o'er those hills
And isles of beauty fill my dreams
Twain would I linger as fresh the air
Fills my desires, and yet it seems.
Scotland, so near and yet so far
Only in mind have I met thee fair
But like my own devoted isle
Like a rock you stand, but do not stir.

*Joan Harris*

## ME

This face that you see,
that's right, the one that I'm reflecting,
that face, the one I'll always show.

Deep inside I'm down and negative,
and you'll never need to know.
To tell the truth, I'm not fussed to live,
and to be frank and honest,
I'm not that interesting to know.

You'd only be glad of my non-existence,
I embrace my invisibility.
Not being acknowledged, ignored,
keeps me detached from humans.
And how uncomfortable you feel as you read each line
(Is it touching a nerve?)
Well, how's this for creativity
These emotions are part of by-product of who we are,
as idle and lazy and balked upon as they are.
With your conditioned, brainwashed attitudes
the likes of me would be labelled crazy.
Pessimism is a gift and happiness does not mean contentment.
Read the words a few times and figure your stuff out.

*J A Carter*

## EMOTIONS

We know we are not immortal
We know that we will die
So why does death surprise us
And bring tears to the eye?

If we believe, and we have faith
We know death is not the end
Then why do we mourn and grieve
When we lose a friend?

Because we're only human
Our emotions run quite high
It's sad to think a loved one's gone
And that is why we cry.

Our families rally round us
But they and friends don't know
The thoughts that we keep hidden
And try hard not to show.

Our memories we'll always have
Though they are hidden too
Reluctantly we'll share some
But they'll be very few.

*M Lyon*

# AIR RAID (CIRCA 1941)

Night begins to fall
Tension starts to mount
The blackout curtains have been closed and checked
the anxious wait begins.
The siren's banshee wail foretells
the battle has been joined.
Searchlights,
pencil-thin against the black of night,
comb the skies
looking for the bombers droning overhead.
Metallic clatter
as the firebombs strike,
desperate men,
with stirrup pump and sandbag,
shouting, cursing,
fight to save their homes.
The chilling whistle of the falling bombs,
the heavy thuds as ack-ack guns respond.
A landmine dangling from a parachute
goes slowly flapping by
A blinding flash
A devastating roar
and the local school has gone.

*G R Bell*

## ANNIVERSARY 2000

The calendar date is born again
and the Lord's Prayer is a landmark,
to remind us of a VIP,
a man above all others
whose stories are still with us.

Whose words became a church,
whose life was led in so much pain,
whose pain reminds us of ourselves,
whose death gave rise to all our shame.

The day grew dark, the sun went down,
old soldiers threw themselves upon his gown.
His disciples became apostles then,
at the moment of his very end.
Already when his life was lost,
they were leaving all to count the cost.

Society now brought to its knees,
praying for forgiveness please,
on the 2000th birthday anniversary,
of someone very special.

*M C Jones*

# THE SUN, MOON AND STARS

When I looked through the window, I could see
Gazed at the night sky
Black as could be.

The moon I saw
Still shone over me
Wherever I go
There it will be.

The diamond stars made me realise,
That some
Things will always be
In our imagination,
Bigger than our conception,
Like a star belonging to my mother
And like the moon in Eire.

In my mind if I feel alone,
I think she can watch me
Through the darkened night
And I am always in and surrounded by life
In its purest form.

The old trees that have seen more than I
And the birds and birds of prey,
True free spirits, flying away,
To far off countries
Before returning this way.

Fish in the sea, in an underwater world,
The grass is a carpet, flowers are its borders,
The animals and the people
The sun, the moon and the stars,
Nature and the planets
Venus, Mercury and Mars.

*Emma Sweeney*

# FORGIVEN

As I lay in wait
Outside the Pearly Gate
Would God let me in?
As I was not without sin.

Plucked from the depths of Hell
From where I fell
Was I redeemed?
Yes it seemed!

An angel came
To hear my claim
That I had done
More good than some.

Yes I had been bad
Yet the times that I had
I had had good cause
Yet I still showed remorse.

God knows that I had faith
Would this reserve me a place
He knows me inside out
So he knows what I'm about.

As I lay in wait
Outside the Pearly Gate
God forgave me my sin
And let me in.

*Andrew John Stevenson*

# FOR THE LOVE OF OLIVER - OUR COCKER SPANIEL

A little ball of fluff
Christmas Eve. A bad, stormy night
My sister came to the home holding Oliver tight.

I wasn't convinced. I wasn't sure I had done the right thing
Should I keep this surprise
Or give Roy a ring.

I took a taxi home surrounded by toys and bones
I cuddled Oliver inside my coat
The kindly taxi man took us home

I crept down the path. Luckily Roy was in the bath,
I pushed this little fella into the room
Oliver was shaking I hoped he would stay
Then I heard Roy say, 'Hello, we've got a stray.'

'Happy Christmas,' I said, 'this is your baby and I've brought his bed.'
Tears came to Roy's eyes - 'This isn't true, it can't be true.'
I said, 'Happy Christmas - he is for you.'
Now Oliver is four years of age,
I should have kept a diary page by page
To read to you how we love Oliver,
From a ball of fluff whose bed was a cage
To a loving animal who has changed our lives forever
Could we leave him - never! Never! Never!

*Carole Umpleby*

## MY SON MARK

From the top of his head
To the tip of his toes
He's loving and sweet, everyone knows
His hair is golden brown
His face is covered in golden down
My son Mark.

What joy fills my soul
How I become whole
When I see my beau
My son Mark.

For him I would climb mountains
For him I should swim oceans
I will not let the tears fall
He would not like me to cry!
I would rather die
Than upset
My son Mark.

*Pat Seddon*

## TOMORROW

Even though the sun may be clouded
In the hurrying pace of life,
Move on for there's always tomorrow,
Darkness will lead into light.

Even though your goal is uncertain
And chaos is all around,
Move on for there's always tomorrow,
Where stillness will abound.

*Angela Dolphin*

# COME HEAR MY CRY

We come from everywhere
And we come from nowhere
Our bodies broken
Minds destroyed
As innocence becomes erased
We are the faceless ones you'd rather forget

We did not choose our position
Nor do we seek retribution
That is for the victim
And yes, we hurt ourselves
Yes, we filled our veins with chemicals
Cut and maimed our skin
Drank ourselves into oblivion

But my friend we stand as witness
To all the horror heaped upon *us*
And those who are no longer here
Touched by the hand of God
We sing a song of innocence
A song of people who will not be hurt again
The power of our forgiveness
Casts shadows over your evil

For we are the survivors
We are the strong
Unbowed and unblemished
Our spirit a beacon of hope
A light in the deepest, blackest night
Shining for those who are no longer with us
And yet have never left us
We come from everywhere
And we come from nowhere
Yes, we are the survivors.

*Kevin Eccleston*

## AFTER

You light two cigarettes,
one for me and one for you.
They dangle from your lip
like a star from the silver screen.

You preen.
I beam.
I know I'm on a supernova,
flying high and bright for now.
Though I know this day won't last . . .

Back to the kids and drudgery.
The mortgage and the war.
The Jacuzzi in the bedroom
and the longed for six-seater car.

The curtains are soon opened,
the clothes are put back on.
The bed is used and spent for now,
hours of passion almost gone.

But I'll see you in the station,
suited, booted, waiting for the train.
I'll nod a quiet 'hello' and pass you by
and swallow up my pain.

*Dawn L Edwards*

# A MAN'S BEST FRIEND

You must have walked through many a park
To sample nature's delights
You must have listened to the lark
And relished all the sights
To smell the flowers and the trees
And fill your head with pleasure
To watch the birds and watch the bees
And sample every treasure
To wend your way down winding paths
Delights round every corner
And watch the birds in little baths
And wondered at the fauna
To see the children running free
Enjoying every hour
And all around you, you can see
How nature shows her power
People fishing in the lake
Escaping life's great pressure
Enjoying life for enjoyment's sake
In breezes warm or fresher
On sunlit days at dusky eve
You walk for hours and hours
You wander till it's time to leave
One last look at the flowers
And now, alas, to leave you choose
Your senses at a height
You notice something on your shoes
Oh dear! It's doggie sh***
(Don't you just love 'em?)

*Charles Henry*

# THE COLOURS OF THE RAINBOW

Pale blue white and summer gold
The animals in the field
You made my heart so full of love
And in it, Your gifts, I know are sealed

Weeds that look like flowers
Grass that grows as green
Butterflies they're made of lace
Pure wonders to be seen

Heart-shaped ivy leaves
That whisper in the night
Evening primrose
With golden leaves so bright

And the sunburst leaves
On tiny plants around
And as the sun it sets
The stars that shine with sound

From one horizon to the other
A picture You painted for me
All the colours in all the world
With love they do surround me

The colours of the rainbow here
The love that You share out
And now, with summer near
Pure pictures, painted everywhere.

*April Dickinson-Owen*

## DISCO DANCER

I watched a young man with a talent rare
Set apart from colleagues who could only stand and stare
As his body twisted, legs and arms askew
Feet moved as if the very floor he graced was moving too
Then his arms, akimbo, quivered in their sleeves
Vibrant as the rich green grasses waving in a meadow's breeze
Forward, backward, leaning, swaying in a stiff disjointed pose
Every muscle lithe and supple, from his shoulders to his toes.
He, himself, a mass of colour, brown and yellow, blue and white
Body bright with perspiration, hair awry and eyes alight.

I watched one of, say, a dozen at a festive fun event
Envied him his gay abandon as girls ogled in delight
Thrilled to gather where his shadow chanced to fall across the floor
Cheered him when the scene was over
Pealed applause and yelled for more
I wished well upon a young man with such power to thrill and please
Hoped he'd find success and riches and that, with the both of these
There would come in equal measure, wisdom for his future ways
And contentment in abundance for the less exciting days
But, for now, the young man's vision guides him ever to the top
With one aim, one sole ambition,
Just to better, 'Body Pop'.

*D J Totten*

## CUMBRIA

I am the singer, living in a song.
The words are old and the melody is strong.
Feel its rhythm in the places I belong,
I am the singer, living in a song.

Lyrics written by the light of breaking day,
As across the lake the darkness fades away.
Sun-topped hills melting down the misty grey,
Lyrics written by the light of breaking day.

*And when I'm away the music still remains,*
*Coursing through my veins - Cumbria.*

Notes are playing from pages, summer green,
Like a thousand summer melodies have been.
Words are clear but who knows what they mean?
Notes are playing from pages, summer green.

Noonday choruses shimmering in the sun.
Waterfalls, cascading rainbows run.
High in blue, the lark's song has begun,
Noonday choruses shimmering in the sun.

*And when I'm away the music still remains,*
*Coursing through my veins - Cumbria.*

Silent shadows on the fell sides start to grow,
And the tempo of the silver beck runs slow.
Holds the memory of the last notes in its flow,
Silent shadows on the fell sides start to grow.

Tomorrow's dawn will sing the song again,
With new meanings and words in the refrain.
Beauty lasting, while nights and days remain,
Tomorrow's dawn will sing the song again.

*And when I'm away the music still remains,*
*Coursing through my veins - Cumbria.*

**Robbie Ellis**

## SELF

I may be just a gardener, no master to my trade
Nothing but a simple man, no job would I evade
I can weed the flower beds, or maybe mow the lawn
Although some tasks be tedious, to never see me yawn
No college education, but words that must be read
My needs, a glass of Adam's ale and butter to my bread
I never longed for riches, nor left this country mine
Never dressed like city gent, not taken out to dine
My road through life be humble, find dirt to my attire
No silver stick nor bowler, this is not my desire
My outlook always cheery, my summer days be long
My winter days be nearing, as each man to his song
When I go home each evening, there's welcome at my door
There's supper on the table, my slippers to the floor
There's cake for tea on Sundays, the kettle sings his song
A cushion for my easy chair, this place where I belong
You may have your country mansion, or castle on a hill
My face may be my fortune, my assets may be nil
I never beg nor borrow, nor take of neighbours' tools
            I may be a simple man
                But live akin the rules.

*A Sheard*

# SPRING

What is a stormy cloud across a new day sky?
Blossom buds awaken in the treetops high
And all the land is softly stirring
In the distance a blackbird, new song he's learning
A warm spring day as winter melts away
What is spring? Daffodils dancing all around the land
Little birds with their nests so grand
Working hard from dawn till dusk
To make new life they really must
Look, a little lamb has just been born
He's shaking his head to greet the morn
Trying to stand on shaky feet, a little lamb, a lamb so meek
Now it's time to do our best, Mother Nature's had her rest
A time to get things done, flowers opening to the sun
Rhododendrons in profusion, everywhere to see
Their beauty takes my breath from me
It's all like a purple haze with a sprinkling of pink and red
A splash of white makes it all a dream
I think there's Heaven in this scene
Newness and colour everywhere, beauty that we can share
Spring.

*Beryl Barlow*

# LIVERPOOL

The city of Liverpool is where I reside
it is in the county of Merseyside
the people you meet
are friendly in the street
and they'll welcome you with arms opened wide.

There's so much to see and do
football, horseracing and the Summer Pops venue
lots of bargains to be found at market stalls
coffee shops and designer gear in the shopping malls
you're guaranteed to come home with a bag or two.

The River Mersey greets the Tall Ships
and the sailors utter many a tale from their lips
museums and art galleries are full of treasures
somewhere interesting to go in all weathers
don't forget the ferry for one of your day trips.

Many cultures living and working as a team
enjoying the city to its full extreme
pubs, clubs and fine eating places
where you'll have lots of fun seeing new faces.
So come for a visit and you'll see what I mean.

*Alison Tichy*

# WHAT AM I?

Here I am sitting alone,
A collection of organs, flesh and bone.
'But what am I really?' I hear you say,
'What makes me unique and have my own way?'

I have lungs and a heart that keep me alive,
And muscles and bones so I can duck and dive.
I have my brain - the control centre of me,
It works all day long as you can very well see.

I also have senses, so I can react to life,
Its sorrows, its pleasures, its blessings, its strife.
My eyes I can use to view the land,
Mountains and valleys, vistas so grand.
My ears I can use to hear wonderful sounds,
Human or other with which nature abounds.
My nose I can use to smell scents in the air,
Some to enjoy, others beware.
My tongue I can use to taste my food,
Bitter or sweet, cooked or brewed.
My hands I can use for pleasure and toil,
My feet, to walk over this wonderful soil.

My heart I can share with friends and others,
Fathers and mothers, sisters and brothers.

My mind I can use, the problems to solve,
The everyday things that around me revolve.

My soul I believe was given to me,
To thank the Lord who has the key.
The gates of Heaven to open wide,
When I leave the Earth for the other side.

My personality I leave you to choose,
Am I a poet or just a muse?

***Nicola Preston  (16)***

## SOLWAY

An open boat, an open sky,
Cirrus swirl of cloud on high
A limitless sea, no land to view,
Lonely peace and serenity.

Long born swell, slow rise and fall,
Billow and hiss of great deep water,
No voice. No call.
Just a whisper of air
And curl of eddy under the quarter.

Blue of the sky and warmth of the sun,
Effortless lift from each coming swell,
A gurgle of tide on its gentle run;
And faintly responding, in the haze to the south'ard
A Middle Ground Shoal buoy clamours its bell.

*John Rowland Parker*

# KELD CHAPEL

Gazing in from outside
Through triple-arched windows,
My view not disrupted
By any stained glass,
Wooden pews in simple majesty,
Like the table's wooden cross.
I enter the church through a doorway
With an age-bent beam across.

Shreds of light glance down,
Spotlights on the ancient flags.
My breath coils out before my face
Diamonds in the air like icy glass.
A breezy draught is curling
Through the blackened fireplace,
Embraced by a Presence of thought,
Surrounded by the aged stones.

In the sun, once more, I turn my face
Towards the winding lane,
And climb away up the sloping hill.
I come to the road's awkward bend,
And stop to gaze back
At the hidden gem.
I have a sense of change about me
And a burst of light within.

*Katie Hale*

## FOREVER ENGLAND

*(Edenside, dawn)*

Dawn; grey with a touch of pink
And lacy mists about the fields and trees;
Cold first as death and with a deathly calm,
Which breaks on song of thrush and lark
As upwards rides the sun in gold and red,
All mingling with the leaves and grass and mists,
And molten gold and amber flows the stream,
A medley of tears and joy down towards the sea,
Towards eternity.

*Jan Courtenay*

## NATURE BOY

I love to walk down a country lane
Where the march of time has halted
And except for seasonal changes
Nature remains unaltered

The birds sing their songs in the hedgerows
As they did in days of yore
And cattle in the meadows munch the grass
An everlasting chore

Then! Down the lane comes a hooting car
Filling the air with gasses
Poisoning the atmosphere
And everything else it passes

I realise that with man's advance
Nature doesn't stand a chance.

*Brian O'Brien*

# THE SHADOW

I've now become a shadow
Lost in space and time
I could have done something
In this wonderful world of mine

People say hello and smile
Stop and talk for a while
I wish I were more than a shadow
In this wonderful world of mine

I wanted to talk about something
Beyond this mundane glass
Sometimes when I feel brave, I wish the mirror would smash
And let me live in this wonderful world of mine

Routine and bills killed off interesting thoughts
Instead I keep busy with life's wonderfully dull chores
That's why I'm a shadow
In this wonderful world of mine

It's great when you stop and see
The most blossomest blossom that could possible be
In that split second I could stop being a shadow
And see, this wonderful world of mine

Intervals where I can see are few
And I want to see what once I knew
Before the blackness of the shadow
Show me this wonderful world of mine.

*Marie Ryder*

## BOCA CHICA:

The bottles are getting warm.
Electricity cut out
A long time ago.
Hurricane.
Sticky clothes,
Sweating won't stop.
The humid air thickens.
Agonisingly slow fan
Drags around.

Open pores on a
Hispanic, picturesque girl.
Rope hammock swings
Gently rocking her.
Fanning with a magazine,
Yet hair clings to shoulders
Oily and bronzed. Sleepy,
She can only wait and suggest
In mutters to her lover.

Droplets worming onto
His scalp, causing itches
And swearing.
He grapples
With wires in the shack corner.
Sand, twigs between toes.
Curbing his language,
Turns to smile at
Woman and child.

*Gillian Ripley*

## EMOTIONS OF THE INDIAN OCEAN

I have my headphones on, listening to my sounds,
here in my hotel grounds.
An Indian experience is what I'm feeling,
the sound of the river and fishermen reeling.
I've only been here now a couple of days,
I've seen so many things, different in so many ways.
I've not been so far yet, but seen so much.
I've experienced sights even a hard heart it would touch.
I feel so tearful yet so joyful, a wonderful mixture of emotion,
I'm so grateful that I have so much more to see amongst
this beautiful Indian ocean.
I'm off out again today to explore some more,
off to a town called Calangute, a busy town I'm led to believe,
I'm stretching my emotions to see what I can achieve.
To explain my emotion would be like having a stomach
full of ocean, it rises, it lowers.
Sometimes rough, sometimes smooth, free flowing, nothing to prove.
If my inner ocean were to rise and reach my throat,
to describe this would be like the riverbanks bursting and flowing
into my eyes, forming my tears, tears of joy, sadness, also laughter,
these tears would be my own to experience, here, now and
forever after.

*Michael Cunningham*

## MEMORIES

Lord, you shine, you're the Creator of mankind.
The trees and lights ring out bright at night
The spirit of Christmas is about, it's our delight
Wake up, wake up, Jesus Christ is about
Snow bells and mistletoe and three cheers
Christmas trees and harmony in sight,
It's our delight. Happy days are here
Saints and sinners rejoice overnight.
Alarm bells ring with Santa, St Nick and our King
Children's eyes open wide, minds of mystery and wonder
Windows sparkling clean, trees, white as snow, so remember
Boys, what can I say? Boys will be boys
Children on sledges, girls' hair in curls and ribbons in their hair
Beautiful coats in red and snowballs with laughter
Hats that said hello and match the splendour
So remember the star at night that brought the good new of
Bethlehem and Heaven and three in the Nativity.
Love is our King, beautiful and majestic,
King of stability, it's time to remember you're mine - *Our Father.*

*Patricia Hampson Curry*

## APPRECIATE YOUR SENSES

I am lying down with my eyes closed.
I can hear a train speeding along in the distance, destination unknown.
I can feel the early morning dew on my face.
My thoughts wander to being christened as a child.
I can hear birds singing in a nearby tree.
I can smell the fragrance of a plant, flower unrecognisable to me.
I can imagine the colour of its petal shapes,
And how delicate it must be.
As I sit up, I feel a moss of some sort,
Spongy and soft to the touch.
I am startled to hear the sound of children's laughter.
I turn around to focus, I can see them playing in a nearby country
                                                    cottage garden.
Oh, how I need to quench my thirst.
It's the first time I've broken down for a while.
But one thing I do know,
It's made me appreciate all of my senses,
And to be a little patient once in a while.

*J Grooby*

# THE CHILD SWEEPERS

Unjustified cruelty
From an early age
Working as sweepers
Without a wage
Sold by parents who were very poor
Some left their families
And were seen no more
Scraps of stale meat
Is all they were fed
They slept on their soot bags
At night in a shed
They climbed narrow chimneys
Their lungs filled with soot
They couldn't wear shoes
So they struggled barefoot
Beaten and threatened
If they refused
Machines could clean chimneys
But children were used
Unschooled and unwashed
How cruel it all seemed
Their life was so dirty
Through chimneys they cleaned.

*Peter Owen*

## EASTER TIME

The glory of the springtime tide,
Heralds Easter time with pride.
Daffodils golden, gently swaying
Nodding heads as though they are praying.
Little chicks and fledglings chirping
Crocus carpets from the ground emerging.
These wondrous repeats of nature's patterns
Sent to remind us of a truth that matters.
Jesus, the Christ, was nailed to His cross
For mankind's redemption of all things past,
The greatest gift that was freely given
So rejoice once more for our Lord is risen.

*Norah Rawlinson*

## SNOWDROPS

If life was a snowdrop,

Where would it land
In a playschool or even in someone's hand?

Many snowflakes have fallen, quietly on the ground.

So please Mr Snowdrop take my hand,
Lead me into paradise land.

Take me by the hand, so I may grow and lead another's hand.

*Deborah Storey*

## COOL AND CLEAR

So this is our new place,
so vast 'n' full of space.
It is so cold at this time of year,
but, I and my buddies, must show no fear.
We're fed up of people looking and staring,
giving us scraps of food, so sparing.
A voice says, 'We've got to build you up slowly'
'Who do you think you are up there, so holy?
funny-shaped objects are left in our home.
Making it cramped 'n' hard to roam.
A gentle voice from above, seems to sing,
'There you go my darlings, see you in the spring.'

***Carol John***

# FIREFIGHTERS OF THE BLITZ

Boldly we go 'neath darkening skies,
through sirens' wails and wardens' cries.
We are immortal! - Without fear,
to those that watch us drawing near.
'Go forward!' they say as they retreat,
then! - Pointing wildly down the street:
'Forward to where the flames do roar
and the smoke is thick - down to the floor.
Go forward and stand with faces stern.
Forget the flames! - Ignore the burns.
Go forward into the jaws of Hell and
the deafening sound of the fire bells.
Go forward! Don't heed the falling walls
or the choking smoke that ascends in palls.
Go forward - ignore the bombs that crash
and the scything cuts as the windows smash.'
So forward I go - with bated breath,
amidst the flames with crackling jet.
My courage? - Put hard to the test
as my comrades urge me on.

*Neil Kelly*

## SUNSET

Ghost pale, he waits upon the hands,
whose fingers touch the shadow lands
and beckon sleep.
She lingers still and casts her eye,
hypnotic as a lullaby,
upon the mirror, where reflected,
sees her burnished heart
of red and gold.
A gaze she cannot hold.
He smiles a crooked smile to see
an echo of tranquillity
adrift upon the inky deep,
where sinking down,
she fell asleep.

*Linda J Liggett*

## HIS GIFTS

Yes, 'Mistletoe and wine', 'Christian rhymes',
From a lovely song, by a modern man;
But these - like 'The Holly and the Ivy' are signs,
Of much greater things, from the distant past.

A man, born in Bethlehem, in Judea,
Into poverty at His birth, in an occupied land, one
Of fear and cruelty, hypocrisy - they be but
Some signs of things to come.

Yes, He lived a good, yes, holy life in Judea.
The ideal son for a poor carpenter,
And his young wife Mary?
And their larger family of sisters and a brother.

But He died a contemptuous way;
Performed by the Romans, after judgement,
                but only after the Pharisee's say
Hung on a cross, with blood and love flowing down,
For you and me and all who may repent.

*ABC*

## The Elephants

If I have been away,
No matter when or where,
I round the corner, head for home
And the elephants lie waiting there.

Sometimes I might encounter them,
When summer's day is gone.
Dark shadows accentuate their giant limbs,
As they rest in the strident sun.
Or in winter, shoulder to shoulder,
Cheek by jowl, their outline bold,
Soft white blankets gently laid across their backs,
For keeping out the cold.

Those who yearn for foreign climes,
When they have had their fill,
Return to find the Howgills
Loyal, constant, still.

*Eileen Todd*

## TURBINE TURMOIL

In our county of Cumbria, yes we are on English soil,
There are panoramic views that people wish to spoil.
Despite all the rolling splendour, of our little-known farming lands,
Plans are about to devastate, our scenery as it stands.

Some bigwigs from the city, have deemed that there should be
Other ways from those we know, to provide our energy.
So now they say they plan to erect, 'without causing any harm'
Huge strange monstrosities to form a large wind farm.

They don't care what devastation their project could entail.
The damage to the environment, the wildlife it could curtail
This day and age nothing seems to halt what people call progress,
The only thoughts are for money, power and success.

The constructions of these turbines, some up to 300 feet.
'Heaven knows how many they may finally complete.'
Will stand out on our skyline, like beings from outer space
Reviled and said by many to be an absolute disgrace.

It doesn't seem to matter, how many people disagree
Or voice objections, expressing their views of the misery
That such a development could easily bring to bear
Upon these small communities, I'm sure they just don't care.

Yet, though one accepts that progress must always go ahead
Coal, oil and water power have all been tried instead
Acceptance will have to be, although it is awfully hard
Why did they have to put them all in our backyard?

*D T Pendit*

## TIME

Time rolls on in an endless flow
Not stopping or pausing for anyone
Just like the tide that comes and goes
It ebbs away at life, no emotion it shows.

The clock ticks relentlessly on
We don't notice the minutes gone
We think we're here for ever and more
But time doesn't, that's for sure.

We can't see or fight this silent foe
As it takes its toll as old we grow
So always remember and never forget
That time moves on without regret.

*Tony Turner*

## FROM THE HEART

V ery deeply loved are you,
A lways, forever, with a love that is true,
L ove that will live through eternity,
E very day, to infinity,
N ight and day
T hrough sunshine and showers,
I n the very darkest hours.
N ew, fresh, as the dawn of each day,
E rnest, forever, my love for you will stay.

*Joan Thompson*

## LOST LOVE

I love him more and more each day
I love him more than words can say
I love him though it makes me sad
I love him - should I feel so bad?
I want him to kiss me
To know that he's missed me
Like I've missed him and his smile
To make my love feel worthwhile.
To feel his arms around me tight
To make everything feel alright
To not be lost or lonely again
Just to know he feels the same.
I want to give him all I have
To make him proud of himself
To make my love stand and shine
And in our hearts - both entwined.
To love you is to lose you - friends we will remain
Though my heart - will never be the same
I cannot hide my fears but hold you in my dreams
Some things happen and happen for a reason!
I know I love you - too much to hide
It remains the love - always inside
From this day on - I'll tuck it away
And keep it for another day.

I love you George,
always. X

*Amanda Weir*

## KNOCK BACK

Beacon of life, and yet so much more
than any person knows. The foundation
of all days. All forms intoxicate
their spacers, whether mellow or sturdy,
able or simple - a drink is always pleasing.

More verse than sport but trends so dear.
Mature, costly age. A fine wine, bold, but stings
the tongue as any paltry potion ever could.
Dark are all snifters, pick-me-ups, and brews;
invoking inclination of grave proportions.

Soft supplement is only truly pleasing.
A seafaring king sipping from a golden chalice,
with whiskey, screaming, staining his throat;
and rocking the boat. No better than
some sap-sucking scum from a gutter stream.

*Isaac Smart*

## A Time In Summer

A brush, a pen, a canvas, a page
a singer, philosopher, poet and sage
minds catching fire by the power of two
a time in summer is coming for me and you

a blue sky and countryside rushing past the car
a lonesome tree stood in a field afar
a gin and tonic and a cow's company
a time in summer for you and me

a note, a smile, a word, a gaze
a song, a voice, a passion ablaze,
a blue, a black and a glowing moon
a time in summer is coming soon.

*Bethan Williams*

## SENSES AWAKENING

Alone. In my room. On my bed.
It's cold on my own.
I can see you in my head,
Smiling as always.

Alone. In my room. On my bed.
Feeling warmer now thinking of you.
I can hear everything you've said,
Softly spoken.

Alone. In my room. On my bed.
Heating up nicely now.
I can smell you near,
Sure is fab.

Alone. In my room. On my bed.
Getting toastier by the minute.
I can taste our first kiss,
Sweet as honey.

Alone. In my room. On my bed.
Nearing boiling point.
I can feel your presence,
Holding me close.

Alone. In my room. On my bed.
Tingling in anticipation.
Then the door opens,
And I explode into your arms.

*Louise Jones*

## LITTLE RAINDROP

Was just a little raindrop
That fell from out the sky
Spilling questions in their millions
For a single answer why?
This tiny little raindrop
Hardly worth a look
Became the ink that wrote the page
And the chapters in life's book
'Tis just a little raindrop
I think escaped God's eye
Who willed to make creation flow
For all of life . . . and I!

*Martin James Banasko*

# I HATE FISHING

There's water in my wellies
and my feet are soaking wet
I was wading through this river
catching tadpoles in my net

The stepping stones were slipppy
I should have took more care
as I slipped I did the splits
and then went flying through the air

I landed by the riverbank
full of green and slimy mud
I missed a branch by inches
I'd have grabbed it if I could

But I guess I'm not that lucky
nothing's gone right for me yet
I've still got to go home, tadpole-free
and tell my mum how I got wet
I hate fishing.

***Chris Thomas***

## HAPPY TIMES

I recall when I was little, the things that made me glad,
It was Sunday nights playing games with my mum and dad.
It was holidays in 'Sunny Wales' (pouring down with rain!)
In our six-berth caravan, playing games again.
Travel cards for our days out, to get us on the bus.
'Cause at a moment's notice somewhere beckoned us
Dad was always getting lost, (but he always knew the way!)
But as I recall, he was good at darts, he played on Saturday.
I remember football in the street, we played goalie in and out,
And going to the park back then, felt like our big day out.
Big skipping ropes that filled the street, from one side to another,
Then pleading with someone to turn it, it was usually our mother.
The summer never seemed to end and life was so carefree,
The happy times I had back then will always be with me.
My childhood days are gone now, but I always will recall,
Some of my happiest moments in life, were spent when I was small.

*Joanne Basnett*

## UNTITLED

I fear . . .
the air is benign cancer
Is breathing and believing
our stupid society
is not seeing
how far removed we are
from our most fearful thoughts,
that it is most important
to find your state
your proper cause:
I see it -
we are made in
the shadow of Christ
unto a world of battle
and the campfire burns
and tells of brotherhood.
Don't you see -
the mountains are
in our hearts
the streams and
the mightiest sea in our soul?
And in the heaven of our mind
is the sky.
We are created to do might,
to thunder out into the desert
to believe and to win . . .
and to love.

*Thomas Conor*

## LIVERPOOL

Out of the ashes a city rose,
from a rich and ancient past.
A tapestry of colour. Her canvas, a
skyline built to last.
Her cathedrals . . . two . . . arise
amidst an ever-growing urban sprawl.

A myriad of cultures form this city
whose history links us all.

The Royal Philharmonic,
modern art and renaissance.
Theatres spawning famous names
of past and present tense.
The music of the 'Beatles''
sense of humour.

A distinctive Mersey sound,
a nasal resonance for which the city is renowned.

Libraries, universities, docklands, now rebuilt.
Football teams of which they can be proud.
St George's Hall, majestic stands,
but above it all the Liver Building soars.
A free port trading world-wide,
reputation is restored.

Tradition's safely anchored on the Mersey's flowing tide.
And so we wait, impatient
For the year 2008.

*Edna Sarsfield*

## OLD AGE

I've spilled soup all down my blouse again
It really is unfair,
I put it on clean this morning
Just after I'd washed my hair
Now it needs washing all over again
And it had only just been pressed
I will have to start wearing a bib again
Then I won't spill things on my dress
I feel so young yet I act so old
Whatever's the matter with me?
My hands start shaking and won't keep still
Whenever I'm drinking my tea
They say you go back to your childhood
I'm beginning to think that's true
I think I'll try a baby's bottle
Next time I make a brew.

*W Atherton*

## HOUSE CLEARANCE

Hold me close
    the dolls have come
        down from the loft.
One by one, dollies dark and blonde
endowed with the warmth of their owner.
Baby dimples, a pink nose
smudged, not by slobber and lots of kissing
but a fine face powder of dust.
Hold me closer, now I know
more sweet things salted away forever
can come back.

To wait in a line, eyes glistening.
Waiting . . . for what?
How to be ruthless?
If there's no answer better watch out!
A huge Humpty Dumpty
a panda, a womble, even worse
    the teddy bears are coming
        down from the loft.
And over there is a dressing-up bag
on it a red straw hat. Easy to smile
at a memory
hard not to cry for old rags.

Here on the landing
hold on.
Hold on to me still
for I see that the teddies are just as soft
and Tiny Tears dressed to kill.

*Gina Riley*

## My Teacher

Eyes like the Devil
Big and round
He's never very happy
And he's not very sound
He's got a head full of nothing
Except for green sheets
He shouts so loud
You fall off your seats
Reflection of the window
Shining on his head
I think he's very boring
I'd rather stay in bed.

*Kelly Gibbons*

## PANIC ATTACK

I'm all shuck up, sweat runs down my forehead
I catch a glimpse of myself in a mirror looking half dead.
So I stand up, the room spins and my legs feel weak
Look in the same mirror, still looking at myself looking like a freak.
So I sit back down, my heart pounds and I don't know what to do
And all this time I'm convincing myself, look James,
                              everyone is looking at you.
I've got to get out of here, this noise is getting to me
What's happening to me, Man, what could this be?
So with that thought I'm down the stairs and out the door
But I don't know how I've got this far because it feels like
                              my feet haven't hit the floor.
So I'm outside, fresh air hits me in the face
I feel sick now and my anxiety level has gone into outer space.
Now I've got cold sweats and I've started to shake
This has happened for years now, you think God would give
                              me a break.
I've started to think now, I've started to calm down.
So it's time to look for a bus, time to get out of town.
Thank God that's gone and I've crossed a line
I've said bye-bye to anxiety, well, until next time.

*James Kitts*

## FRIENDS ARE LIKE ANGELS

Friends are like angels,
Who brighten up our day,
In all kinds of wonderful and magic ways.

Their thoughtfulness comes
As a gift from above,
And we feel surrounded
By warm caring love.
Like upside down rainbows,
Their smile brings the sun
And they fill ho-hum moments,
With laughter and with fun.

Friends are like angels,
Except with no wings,
Blessing our lives
With so many precious things.

*Vicky Tam*

# COULD I BE WRONG

Why don't you stay in bed tonight
Instead of walking the floor?
Why won't you take notice
Instead of slamming the door?
That temper of yours won't help you,
If you have to go away,
And once you go, I'll not have you back,
Not even for a day.
I can't understand what's wrong with you,
I wish you'd been born a lad
Then it might have been different,
It wouldn't have been so bad,
We've bent over backwards to please you.
You have to admit that it's true.
Just because I won't give in to your temper
Your behaviour is getting worse
Your mother couldn't handle you,
That's why she asked me to nurse,
Stop screaming and crying in your bedroom,
Or people will start to complain.
You haven't got appendicitis, but you're giving me a pain!
If I sent for the doctor, you'd probably laugh with glee
But if you did, it would be the last time,
That you'd make a fool out of me!

*James Ayrey*

# THE MEANING OF LIFE

The whistle sounds
A hush descends;
Not a sound
From either end,
The ball is placed
The goalie waits
The striker stands
And concentrates . . .
He takes a breath
Pulls up his socks
Whilst on the line
The goalie rocks,
His eyes flit left,
Then right then up,
Then down and then . . .
He eyes the Cup!
He lifts his head
Takes two steps back
He takes a run
His leg swings - *whack!*
The crowd erupts
Some boo some cheer,
The striker grins from ear to ear
The ref decides
The time is up
The better team
Has won the Cup!

*Joanne Cross*

## YOU

I look at you
and smile inwardly
the kind of smile
reserved for lovers

I look at you
and as our eyes meet
I want to tell you
how I feel
but instead
I smile a smile
of friendship

I look at you
and want to
show you my trust
and share every past
emotion, hoping you
would understand

I look at you
want to kiss you
wrap my arms
around you
feel the length, breadth
width and depth of you

I look at you

*Carlene Montoute*

# A MORTAL BLOW

A special thought in my head,
I think of him when I'm in bed,
He passed away when I was young,
Because of cancer in his lung,
His love is in my heart every day,
I wish he hadn't gone away,
My dad.

*Katy Flynn  (12)*

## HIGH AND ABOVE

The 'Tree Pipit'
Anthus trivialis
Has
'A singing habit for a tall tree'
He needs a tall tree to finish his song!
She builds a nest on the ground,
They feed amongst the roots
Amidst the soil they feed
But
Trivialis has an aerial song
Anthus trivialis needs a tall, tall tree to finish its song.

*Irene Clare Garner*

# TIME

Like the froth of a cappuccino
As the ferry passes
Leaving tracks
Like distant roads
Going on and on until a point
Then stops
And fades away as time passes by
Then suddenly there is no trace
Of a huge creature passing
It's just forgotten about
Like a brass band playing a march
When the waves crash violently
Across the snow-capped rocks
Never to be seen
    Or heard of
        Again.

*Stacie-Nicolle Mortimer  (13)*

# FISH IN THE SEA

They say there are many fish in the sea,
But I have chosen you!
This day you are standing in front of me,
So wishes *do* come true!

You don't look like a fish to me,
You look like a pretty girl!
And when I gaze at your good looks,
My mind is a frenzied whirl!

When your eyes meet mine, there's a flash of light,
That's hard to understand!
I gasp for breath and my heart beats fast,
Your love is now in demand!

When your fingers run right through my hair,
Time should never be at its end.
And when I'm held in your soft embrace,
It's a snowball-type of trend!

You are now mine in holy matrimony,
This day I give thanks to my Lord!
Inconceivable is life without you now,
Your love I shall ever applaud!

We have all our lives in front of us,
I'm pleased to contemplate.
Just a single day with you is bliss,
So a life sentence is just great!

Now that you are my very own,
I don't care for the sea.
Just you stay with me from now,
That is my heartfelt plea!

***Umar Azam***

# THE RUNAWAY

The winter sun was sinking
Casting shadows o'er the land.
Night-time came a'creeping.
Tightening vision like a band.
The snow outside was glistening
In the last light of the sun,
Fading like the thaw
Now darkness had begun.
The candle's flickering glow
Cast spectres around the room.
Creaking from the rafters
Added terror to the gloom.
I sat curled up on the floor
In my sleeping bag all torn
Wishing that I was back home
By the rising sun of the dawn.

*Carole J Fury*

## PREMONITION

The alley slowly choked on the thick, misty fog,
The moon barely visible through the shadowing smog,
I touched the wall, heard a distant cry,
Rain fell from the cloudy sky.

I started shaking, took shorter breaths,
Eyelids lowered, began to sweat,
Bright, white lights blinded me,
I couldn't think, I couldn't see.

The future flashed before my eyes,
Would someone say their last goodbyes?
I felt the fear, I felt the fright,
Would this person last the night?

The premonition seemed so clear,
A window to the future here,
Through my eyes I had the power,
To witness man's final hour.

A figure appeared in the dark,
My mind saw nothing but an empty park,
A woman ran with a chilling fear,
Within her eyes two burning tears.

Her fingers cold, an icy blue,
A bony man struggled through
The fog too strong, a fighting force,
Would this demon show remorse?

Fire appeared in the demonic palm,
The park lit up, a deadly calm,
A passer-by would never see
A drastic death, about to be.

The demon threw the ball of flame,
The woman's heart was where he aimed,
She screamed and fell and hit the floor,
Her life was gone for evermore.

The premonition quickly fades,
I stood there feeling slightly dazed,
Could I change it? Could I help?
I heard another distant yelp.

Somewhere in the park ahead,
I now know a woman's dead.

*Laura Howarth-Kirke*

# JOY

I carefully guarded
Some sweet memories
And kept them within me
To take through my life

You tried your hardest
To take them from me
And smothered the laughter
With wet, heavy strife

I hear the voices
Of my sweet babies
Eternally children
They play in my dreams

Your troubled mind
I take to the Lord
And ask His forgiveness
For all your schemes

And the joy in my life
Was always waiting
For me to find it
In this place I belong

I'm carefully guarding
All of my memories
And making some new ones
As I go along

Each day is a blessing
Since I found true love
And now I'm contented
A so happy boy

So when my Lord asks me
What I did with my life
I'll open my heart
And pour out the joy.

*Paul Shipley*

## EARTH

I often look around and feel like I don't belong,
I feel like an alien when I realise this world is all wrong,
People dying from wars, grudges that never ever end,
Children starving to death with only themselves to depend,

Pollution all around us, we breathe it in every day,
We are killing our planet in every possible way,
Slaughtering animals to make money till they are nearly extinct,
One minute they're here and then gone in a blink,
Forests are cut down, acres at a time,
We must come to a stage where we finally draw the line,

They say we can make our own choices and have freedom of speech,
But this is a lie, all of us are weak.
They say terrorists are evil, brainwashed by their belief,
So we strike back with violence, trying to force the peace,
Propaganda and lies told by our world leaders,
Making us hate each other with the bullshit they feed us,

We are now trying to make contact with intelligent alien life,
But surely we can see this will only bring us strife,
For we can't live in peace, our world is in pieces,
So imagine how we would discriminate against a totally
                                        different species,

No one owns our planet unless there is a creator,
But we still haven't proved this, over 2000 years later,
So what about what I want and many people alike
Who want to live in peace and accept everyone's beliefs
                            as their basic human rights?

Different cultures and races make our Earth an interesting place,
If we all were the same, our brains would go to waste,
So let's join together before it's too late,
For I know death and destruction doesn't have to be our fate.

We take life for granted when it's truly a miracle,
Turn away from power and look to the spiritual.

*Lynsey Gill*

## RING

Sitting beside the telephone waiting for it to ring.
When am I going to hear from him?
'I'll give you a call next week to fix up our next date.'
If he doesn't ring soon, I shall go ape.
The first call, my mum.
'Just ringing to see how you are.'
Get rid of her quick, cut the conversation short.
Find things to do around the house, keep busy, lift my spirits.
Housework can be good for the soul!
Look at the washing up in the bowl.
Come on, ring, pick it up, test if it's still working.
At last, that magical sound.
'Excuse me, Madam, you fancy a new fitted kitchen?'
I can't believe this, she must be joking!
Why is it when you are waiting for one person to ring, every
Tom, Dick and Harry decide to call?
Eleven o'clock, it's too late, I'm not staying up for his sake.
Snuggled up in bed, drifting off into a doze,
I hear a murmuring.
Pick up the phone.
'Hi, babe, how you doing?'
'I'm in bed, too tired, better leave it until morning
I'll give you a ring!'

*Joy Ottey*

## SAINTHOOD

God's whisper,
to come to me -
you must see me before you die
and when you have seen me
you will see in my realm of reality
that you have died.

I,
eventuality is my drop
of the ocean that I must drink.

Desolate I am of the love
that I knock on God's door
for self-obliteration.

*Adhel Azad*

## MANCHESTER 3000: PLANNING REPORT

There would be problems here for archaeologists,
and the mounds of Manchester are unlikely to reveal
the treasures of a Tel Amarna. The city structure,
or what remains of it, is muddled and confused.

Antique computer records show that Nynex,
and the Gas Board, Water Companies,
and suchlike bodies regularly dug up roadways,
shuffled all the strata. Peripatetic holes
disturbed the sewers, and confused
the ordered structure of the streets.

There are still remnants of broad carriageways,
which history tells were used by cars,
and tram tracks still run underneath the tarmac,
among the cobbles they called setts.

Elsewhere, however, there is other
more confusing evidence of trams
replacing railways. Concrete rafts,
(like artefacts unearthed at Swindon)
show signs of overpainting, as do humps
set round with small brick blocks
along the streets. Carbon dating shows
that these were of a later generation
than those beneath the streets.

All this is interesting, but the needs
of modern citizens must come before
such sentimental histories. Therefore,
we would recommend that these remains
are not worth preservation, and that
construction of a modern transport system
can go ahead.

*Elizabeth Parish*

## SAINT PETER'S SQUARE, MANCHESTER

In this Square,
the sculptures speak of peace.
The library,
based on a Roman pantheon,
is dominant and domed,
round and solid,
a contented grandmother
keeping watch.

She sees a long white caterpillar
nudging along,
collecting commuters,
from business or play.
Past the Midland Hotel,
of terracotta stone,
its gold-edged steps,
a very far cry
from days gone by,
when sixty thousand people
in Saint Peter's field,
fought for cheaper bread.
Four hundred were wounded,
eleven were dead.

In this Square,
when the light has nearly gone,
and the cenotaphs stand tall
against the Manchester sky,
the poppies are wreathed
dark in the gloom.

*Edith Ward*

## THE MAN SITTING UNDER THE TREE

There's a man sitting under a tree in a garden.
I wonder what he's thinking.
He's sitting in the shade,
looking pensive.
It's a hot day.
He just sits there.
He's not sunbathing.
The sun beats down on the garden path.
The weather's very warm.
He just sits there on the bench,
gazing at the lawn.

*Rachel Van Den Bergen*

# ROLLER COASTER

Up and down, and round and round,
*Clickety-clackety-clack,*
A million miles above the ground,
*Clickety-clackety-clack,*
Higher! Higher! To the top!
Your tummy tightens, your ears go pop!
And down so fast, you just can't stop!
*Clickety-clackety-clack.*

Loop-de-loop and round the bend,
*Clickety-clackety-clack,*
Down the slope at G-force ten,
*Clickety-clackety-clack,*
Falling downwards from the sky,
Watching people whizzing by -
So this is what it's like to fly!
*Clickety-clackety-clack.*

One more lap around the track,
*Clickety-clackety-clack,*
Forward! Forward! Then go back!
*Clickety-clackety-clack,*
There's nothing more I'd like to do,
Than sit this ride sat next to you,
Feeling high and feeling blue;
*Clickety-clackety-clack.*

***K Baskin***

## THE REMNANTS OF WAR

The legacy of war, hate and crime
Has marred our society
In these troubled times.
So many guns on our streets
Killing off our nations,
Without even shoes on their feet.
Too much blood has been shed
So many times people have gone to bed without bread.
Our fellowmen have forever been fighting,
For what they believe in.
But how can they achieve it
If there is no surrender?
Far across the land,
And across the sea,
Dreams of making life better
It seems wasn't meant to be,
Only to be shattered by the threat of war.

People moving from one place to the next.
Acting as if they are hexed.
They seemed to turn into nomads overnight.
Scurrying along, in a flurry of flight,
With their only belongings strapped to their backs,
Feeling lost and confused
As the sun beat down on their backs
Weak and subdued, disorientated and bewildered
They made their way to a land
That seemed lost and unknown.
A land that was far, far away from home.

With their weather-beaten faces
And their mud-splattered feet,
They begged for deliverance
From hunger and defeat.

And as they pitched their tents
On the highways and byways,
Knowing not what lay around the corner,
Dreading to think what lay ahead.
Tired and weary, faint and disillusioned,
Showered in misery and humiliation,
Here remains the remnants of war.

*Dellis Barracks*

## FOR A FRIEND

It's so very hard knowing what to say
Or to understand just why
Why did he have to go away?
Why did he say goodbye?

But for now and for every day
Don't be afraid to cry
As in our hearts he will always stay
So hold your head up high.

*Peter James Cox*

## MY STARS

They're my stars,
My home from home,
The ones I look at when I'm alone.
When I see them,
I have no fear,
They always remind me,
My home is here.

***Colin Horn***

## REMINISCENCE

I remember back in the summers of old
When I was Sir Knight, gallant and bold
The brave captain of HMS climbing frame
Those hot days when life was a big game

I remember those walks with all my family
Those lazy days, the rickety house in the tree
Out playing with mates till late in the park
Days lasted forever and it never got dark

I remember holidays away with my grandparents
Sister and I in the garden making chair tents
The sun beating down, melting our ice creams
Lying in the grass, absorbed by the daydreams

Now those days have gone, a distant memory
Those days where we were happy and carefree
Life moves on, everything we love fades away
Like the summer season, it all ends some day.

*Adrian Salamon*

## THANK YOU
*(A poem for Mum)*

For all the rights and wrongs you taught me
I thank you
For the love and hardships of my youthful days
I thank you
For the little things you taught,
Like blowing bubbles from my tongue and the alphabet backwards
I thank you
For the memories and warm feelings
I thank you
For the love, care, laughter and tears
I thank you
For the strength, pride, encouragement and support
I thank you
For my sisters and brother
I thank you
For the priceless gift of life
I thank you
But most of all for knowing you
I thank you.

*Lisa Killeen*

## THE HOUR

The island we seek on the horizon -
now the mist shrouding us finally gone
. . . ghostly headland . . . many a standing stone . . .

Avoid this jutting rock! Stinging sea spray!
Drag our boat up the beach - then find the way
to that austere place where saints used to pray -

Oblivious of all spirits around
of those who raised stone circles on the ground
or who tunnelled sometimes deep underground -

An island they knew was a sacred place
where each to sun or moon could turn a face -
- wonder about fate in his time and space.

Even when pirates came here to attack
more often than not, they came sailing back.
Of their galleys between islands, no lack.

The settlers partook of each island mood -
farmed inland, fished the sea - well understood
the eerie hour when sky and ocean brood.

We see their homesteads open to the sky.
No one lives here now and we wonder why -
The only sound a raucous seabird's cry.

Birds dive near us, resenting our presence -
yet a greater hostility we sense
from all the Unseen Ones who wish us hence.

So, as men no longer in harmony
with an island so steeped in mystery,
we descend to our boat, in a hurry.

*C M Creedon*

# MUSIC TO THE EARS

Music is the key to peace
It holds the power for hate to cease.

It brings men together in harmony
A brief insight into what could be.

Although temporary, it is a start
To unite men from worlds apart.

A gift of song as sweet as the bird
As powerful as the spoken word.

A song expresses what you would like to say
It can be heard by those with that privilege taken away.

A life is so precious, one I would hope to save
Music is with us from cradle to grave.

Many a man will die for country and king
All will pray that for them the angels will sing.

*L E Marchment*

## GOD IS MY STRENGTH

God is my strength, when the way is hard,
God is my strength, when the sky is dark,
God is my strength, when I feel despair,
    He always comforts me.

God is my strength when I can't cope,
He throws me a lifeline, He throws me a rope,
He lifts me up from the trials of life,
He carries my burden, He eases my strife,
    He always comforts me.

God is my strength when I feel the pain,
He takes my hand, and says, 'Get up again.'
He tells me the sunshine, follows the rain;
    He always comforts me.

God is my strength for a better 'today',
He takes all my trials, and throws them away,
He smiles as He tenderly, looks my way.
    He always comforts me.

*Ann Margaret Rowell*

# LAUGHTER

We should have laughter,
so, let there be laughter,
make a day when
the grinning at your core
helps tomorrow's hope
gurgle through the pebbles
on our bellyaching shore.
Shoo out the witches, bring in the clowns,
open the gates to all of our towns,
let there be laughter.

Purple heather the moors,
bring back the sheep
to everyone's downs;
kick out the politics
and estate-agent hype,
bring back the children
on three-wheeler trikes.

The old year is gone now,
so, let it be;
take tea in the garden,
sit under the tree.
Where now there is morning
don't anticipate gloom,
for today is after,
we must welcome the moon
and bring back the laughter.
Please, please,
bring back the laughter.

*Jim Rogerson*

## BETTER TIMES

If I could make time stand still
Now as I write this letter
I would look after all the children
And old folk I would treat better
I have seen bad things in my life
And it makes me wonder why
There are children who've done nothing wrong
Yet they are going to die
Just think about their suffering
And ask yourself why
As you look into their eyes
It makes you want to cry?
We must reach out to ease their pain
If only for a while
There's nothing that looks better
Than to see a young child smile.

*C E Kelly*

# THE DUSTY CRY

What have we learnt from two world wars?
An easier way to settle scores.
Quicker ways to kill the foe,
With marching feet we onward go.
New chemicals to stop the mass,
Guns and bombs that fire and blast.
How chaotic are our lives?
The fear of death won't make us wise.
Where is this land, the victor said,
Was fit for heroes, they're long dead.
Promises made long ago,
To broken men who fought the foe.
In trenches filled with water deep,
Sat weary men, who couldn't sleep.
Do we know, or do we care,
About the ones once slaughtered there?
Many years have passed since when
Our King called out for able men
To come and fight for liberty,
And do their bit to make man free.
But from the dust we hear the cry,
Of those who marched away to die.

Christos

*May Foreman*

## GUN

Just one quick pull
And it's all over
Once loaded
Blood has to be shed
Taken alive or dead
This object gives strength and power
It demands power
This feeling of power is incredible
It is a power in itself
It has the power to harm
It has the power to kill
One to a hundred to a thousand
It must have its fill
This little contraption of pure steel
No bigger than my hand
It is a killer
It is a war machine
It is death itself
It is a lethal machine
Commanding blood
Wanting blood
Demanding blood
It must have its fill
Till the time draws near
It shakes then aims!
It draws; it fires
The smoke quietly fades away
Leaving death behind,

It has had its fill
That is till the next time
This deadly death machine
Needs and wants to have its fill
Then the ritual goes on and on and on
There is no stopping it
It has had the taste and wants more
*More* and *more* and *more.*

**M Sheikh**

## TROUGH OF BOWLAND

Hills behind hills behind hills,
green, peat-dark, grey-blue hazed,
rising and receding in
an illusion of infinity.

Out of a golden sky
the sun sets incessantly
behind high shoulders,
resurrects when ramparts
fall away, dies again.

The road bucks and shies
round bases in drunken curves,
sense of direction dissolving
with the car swing,
the switchback fall and rise.

This is a zone that
seems devoid of human kind,
a precipitate kingdom
of sheep and rugged boulders,
divided up by grids.

Rams with raised horns
or lowered heads
are letting us pass.

*Tim Hoare*

## DESIRE

Heat sears from glaring lights,
blazing on the canvas.
He stands in his corner, alert,
the waiting interminable.
Seconds bicker across his shoulders,
barking instructions, grunting advice.
He stays aloof, switching off.
They'd never understood him.
It wasn't just the money,
or the girls,
or the adulation.
Deep down, that didn't matter.
Nice, but not important.
Only winning mattered,
nothing else would do.
Only winning quelled the hunger,
which burned inside his belly.
Slaked the thirst which screamed,
inside his soul.
Crushed those fears which filtered,
through his brain.
The ball clangs loudly.
He strides forward with caution,
mind and body focused.
The hint of a smile,
forming on his lips.

*Paul Kelly*

## EVIL DREAD

This unholy atrocity
On platform two Madrid
Harrowing. Devastating.
Grief, unbelievable grief
How can this be true?

Al-Qaeda terrorists
Cowards hiding from view
No glory for them
But infamy, murder and blood
Where is the justice in this?

Parents now gone
Brothers, sisters
Daughters and sons
One thousand injured, hundreds dead.

Is there no justice
For the people of Madrid?
This is not God's work
But the work of evil
For God said, 'I am a merciful God
Let my people go, for it is my law
Thou shalt not kill'.

And the law must make this justice
For the people of Madrid
And man's peace
That man may heal
And feed the nations
Then God can say, 'Truly I am your God.'

*Raven*

# IMMUNE

The mudded girl crouches to my eye's line
Washed with a bruised tan beneath the clouds pulped
Runic letters ordering attendance:
She snaps each heel into a leap and scratches my chest
Dropping guiltless blood onto the peat-castled trestles holding the bank
My inanimate lids are reeled for pleasure
As Jennifer lowers to the ground tighter, sniffing for the
                                        abandoned heat
The fission of wood separates me in halves
Forcing abstinence into the centreless work of love;
I must ride lowly in a gunmetal mat wheelchair
Spokes beneath the somatic air of June
Squeezing the life from the hopping green of her eyes and throat
By the lake, eyed by sparrows
Till dusk cradles me in a choric meander
Suckling its sparkling blankets.

*Andrew Gibson*

## A PRAYER FOR BRUCE WAYNE

Perching upon rooftop's edge
As fate o'erlooks its prey,
A winged shadow reaches down,
Bitterly feeling all around
For its tragic past to slay -
A nightly, suffocating pledge.

Childhood torn through hopeful eyes:
Murder stole from parents' love
Its darkest thirst, a seed of blood,
Ne'er to die as vengeance should;
A peace lost to the crying dove -
Blind, a cursed bat would rise.

The weight of an empire promised
In passage to their manly heir,
Begotten for this Gotham prince:
Lonely, shiv'ring in warm mist
At parents' graveyard of despair,
Ne'er to leave or pray there since.

Two sides adorn a golden mask,
One of lineage sparkling, kind,
A daily philanthropic urge;
Yet inside haunts a tortured task,
One of vengeance flooding mind,
A nightly misanthropic purge.

Bruce Wayne hungers, feeding upon
Cancer of Gotham, evil as grey,
A creature of lonely appetite;
Batman lives here as chaos' son,
Rising grim from crime's decay,
A soaring symbol of the night.

*Robert B Appleton*

# THE APPEAL

Exaggerated family secrets are
frowned or smiled at behind a
row of tired tongues that claim
to have heard it all.

She exits the room containing
ingrown words wrapped with desire
pawned needlessly for a cause she knew
could never be won.

Later, it wasn't the vodka she
blamed for her PTA
pole dancing pastiche but
her unremembered disloyalty.

*Debbie Morgan*

## MY MELANCHOLY WISH

Death is not an end but a beginning
That is how the saying goes.
But a saying holds no comfort
To those of us wearing funeral clothes.

When it is our nearest and dearest
The pain is often too intolerable to bear.
Then our outlook on the future
Becomes one of hopelessness and despair.

So my father I weep for you,
With my heavy heart I grieve.
Without your strong guiding hand
I find it difficult to believe.

I no longer hear your words of encouragement
I am deafened by the silence death brings.
I have a trust to the infallibility of memory
And the rosy tint that passing time puts on things.

Now the only thing that is my heart's desire
Is I wish that all our wishes could come true.
Then my dear departed father,
I would be standing here with you.

*Keith Tissington*

## NEVER WILL I LEAVE YOU

Christians, Christians, far and near,
My God keep you in His tender care,
May He lift you up when you fall,
Answer you, when you call;
To grant the request of your prayer,
And to give you grace in your despair.

Christians, Christians, far and wide,
Look to Christ, in Him confide;
When stormy winds seem not to cease,
May He grant you His eternal peace;
For when your feet begin to slide,
He'll be your refuge in which to hide.

Christians, Christians, near and far,
Look to Christ, the bright morning star;
For when the days seem rather dark,
Watch and wait, listen, hark;
For a child of God indeed you are,
Which nought can taint, tarnish or mar.

O Christians, Christians, saved by grace,
Where'er thou art, and in what place;
Christ in thee, His spirit sown,
Christ in thee, thou art not alone;
Though at times, of Him there seemeth no trace,
Yet ne'er give up, but seek His face!

*Ray Varley*

## FOR THE LOVE OF OUR PLANET

Who are they who are taking it apart,
This planet of ours, indiscriminately?
Exposing well-loved traditions to scorn
Creating cultural cul-de-sacs out of it all.

New politics dictating the direction
Reaching out beyond the boundaries of state
Toss the ingredients into the pot
A recipe for disaster, too much haste.

Stout oaks of England growing old
Supplemented by the eucalyptus tree
Changing landscapes, Tesco stores overseas
Choking roads, by-product of the guzzling car industry.

The lanes of placid quietude
Hedged by bramble-bearing bush
Precious refuge for the troubled soul
Where sanity is restored, and fears are softly hushed.

Can we avoid a collision course?
What will it take to turn things around
That each one loves his fellow man?
Put the planet first, for the survival of us all.

*Lyn Wilkinson*

# THE POET'S DAWN

I slowly rise
From my ashes
Oh! My dark past
How it lashes.

Like noble slave
I feel their blows
And remember
Every face
Every word
Every deed
That has been done.

I will arise
From my ashes
And claim my crown
Of laurel leaves,
Rule my domain
With love-power.

Benevolent
Ruling monarch
Of my own life
Of my own thoughts
My own feelings
Own sensations
Forevermore.

*Trevor De Luca*

## UNTITLED

Five little toes sit in a row,
The biggest is called my big toe.
Then next to him is middle toe
And the one at the end is little toe.
All in a row they sit and wait
For their big mystery date,
Here he comes, Mr Heel himself
To collect his toes
For his big date.
The toes and heel become as one.
Mr and Mrs Foot they're now known as
To you and everyone.

*Tracey Dixon*

## ME

I looked in the mirror and what did I see?
Someone that wasn't even me!
I tried to find something in my mind,
But all my thoughts were left behind,
Left behind when you abused my trust,
And took with that all of my lust.
So now, when I look at me,
I don't know what I expect to see!

*Janette Dann*

## THE DANCE AROUND THE SUN

When I watch the sun go down
You cannot see what I can see
So many hands stretching out
All wishing they were you or me.

They are all around that ball of fire
They now do the Devil's dance
If they could right what they did wrong
There is no second chance.

The ten commandments in the book
They all knew good from bad
I hear the song that they all sing
So very, very sad.

If only they had faith in God
And took care of His dear son
And felt the love and care He gave
There would be no dance around the sun.

And even now I walk the land
And tell all it's not too late
All they need is faith in God
To pass through Heaven's gate.

*A F Mace*

## LOST IN TIME AND SPACE

While walking through the country park,
Quite close to my address,
I saw a grey-haired gentleman
In obvious distress.

Now, being such a caring soul,
I went to offer aid.
He thanked me for my kind concern,
And this is what he said.

'I'm nearly eighty years of age,
Been widowed many years.
I was left distraught and lonely,
The worst of all my fears.

Then, last year I met a lady,
So charming, full of life,
She's fifty years my junior,
And she is now my wife.

She's really made me live again
And cooks exotic meals.
She's pretty, loving, faithful,
And cares for all my needs.

The reason why I'm so upset,
When life's so much to give?
My memory has failed again -
I've forgotten where I live!'

*Brian M Wood*

# AND SO THE WHEEL TURNS

Wrapped with warmth secure in all
unaware of your impending fall
fate's dark shadow stretches tall

And so the wheel turns

Plummeting down life's dark well
shocked surprise that you fell
landing in this screaming hell

And so the wheel turns

Slowly climbing back to life
tattered fingers times of strife
memories cut like a knife

And so the wheel turns

Now in the sun life anew
secure in knowing what to do
a little wiser oh! Poor you

And so the wheel turns

Wrapped with warmth secure in all
unaware of your impending fall
fate's dark shadow stretches tall

And so the wheel turns

*Simon Martin*

# DEATH HAS NO MEMORY

Death has no memory
Its occupation has always been known
It walks silently among us
And touches our hearts with a hand of bone

Death has no memory
Yet most of us fear it so
That we strive to push ourselves further
Than our lives would normally go

Death has no memory
Or so I've heard them say
They speak of it in hushed tones
And hope it will stay away

But if death really has no memory
Then why do we fear its tread?
Perhaps we'd rather be afraid
Than in the ground, cold and dead.

*Christopher M David*

# DAD

*(In loving memory of Andy 'Nipper' Bazley. Loving dad, husband, brother, son, nephew, cousin and friend)*

Dad I never said I love you
I never even said goodbye
I've been wondering why
Why you had to die

I wasn't near you when it happened
I wasn't even at home
I'm glad to know that
You're not up there on your own

I'll keep the memories
When we had a lot of fun
Don't forget you have five daughters
And an only son

Kim, your wife, Ted, your dad
Phyllis, your mother
Barbara and Jean, your sisters
Eddie and Phil, your brothers

I'm sorry I wasn't your ideal daughter
I'm sorry we used to row
Don't forget to get me mum back
After what happened to your eyebrows

***Tash***

# HE IS NOT DEAD, BUT SLEEPING

'He is not dead, but sleeping!'
How those words console me,
Speaking of a mystery beyond me,
Almost too much to bear.

And yea, though I lie in the darkness at night
Damp pillow beneath me,
The words they comfort me,
And provide a place in my imagination
Where he can still be.

The day of the funeral a dragonfly darted around us.
Iridescent wings shimmering in the dappled sunlight under the trees.
Fragility itself, and so unearthly bound,
Like a soul set free at last.
Then I could say gladly and feel how my heart lifted,
'He is not dead, but sleeping!'

Since then I often gaze down at the place where he is lying,
As if my eyes could bore down through the very soil.
I speak words as if there is some cosmic mobile phone connection
To take them down,
But where he is I do not want to go!
Two years have gone - I dread what I would find there,
And deep down inside me, like a grave,
In some deep, dark core of my being,
That pragmatic, logical, no-nonsense place,
That 'call-a-spade-a spade', realistic place that rarely sees the light of
day
(And would dismiss it anyway!)
I know . . .
'He is dead, not sleeping!'

*Jane Hinchcliff*

## HOT SUMMER NIGHT

The summer night squats on the house roof
Like a gigantic mother blackbird
Brooding with suffocating fervour
Stifling her suburban clutch

The air hangs thickly outside the window
Like cheap toffee melted and misshapen
From hot pocket-dwelling far too long

Only an occasional breeze
Can slice through the sticky heat
Piercing the heavy air
Like birdsong at dawn.

*Elizabeth M Rait*

## THE LONELY DEMON

The lonely demon
Tonight it flies
With murder and hatred
In its blood-red eyes
Waiting and wondering
For the next victim to bite
Hoping now
That day turns to night
It flew past my window
Late last night
And offered me an offer
Of eternal life.

*Wesley James Byrne*

## TENDER LOVE, SWEET KISSES

Your warm, tender love
And soft, sweet kisses
Are worth more to me
My sweet Linda Marie
Than every single diamond
In a king's royal crown
And your sparkling blue eyes
And wide, bright smile
Fill both my heart and life
Full of love and happiness
And so every time I hold you close
Look into your angel-blue eyes
And kiss your sweet angel lips
My heart beats faster and faster
And my happy spirit flies
Higher and higher
Up into the cloudless sky above
And I feel so lucky and thankful, Marie
To have you in my life
As a very good friend
And my tender, loving wife.

***Donald John Tye***

## SONGBIRD

No harmony, no melody, no song can compare
To the sound of the songbird so pure and so true
As he sings in the trees, as he wings through the air
The soul of the poet his voice does imbue.

His song transforms gloom into something so vernal;
His notes they are pristine, impassioned each tune -
The songbird, so truly a creature supernal,
Illumines my mind like an internal moon.

*Teresa Kelly*

## WHERE IS THE CHILD?

Not enough time, not enough space,
time is short for the human race.
Too much need and the greed for power,
is turning the Earth and the human race sour.

Where is the child of long ago,
who was born to be and not to know?
He sleeps in his cradle, the miracle, born,
his innocence waning, with each new dawn.

No child is born with a cruel streak,
that trait is nurtured week by week.
He quickly learns in this world of sin,
while the purple power is slithering in.

His innocence gone through television,
as commercial break brings indecision.
Where is the child we knew so well,
the three-year-old, not the infidel?

Is he part of a mob in a gang disruption,
heading for terror, bringing destruction?
Oh where is that babe of long ago,
is he driving the car with the bomb below?

*Carole A M Johnson*

# TALENT FROM BIRTH

Hopping from one subject to another,
With entertaining brain, nothing can stop her.
It is rather inviting - keeps her readers alert,
She is here, she is there, grasshopper expert.

Dancing from one haiku to another,
With love's old refrain, rhythmic pentameter.
Words so exciting, bring laughter and mirth,
She is near, she is dear, of poetical worth.

Rictas on love, her father and mother,
April in the rain, Hawaii in summer,
The moon as it shines, from Heaven to Earth
She is sweet, she is neat - a talent from birth.

*Joyce Hemsley*

## A Day Out In Whitby

We went out on a fine day
To splish-splash in the turquoise bay.
We found a boat and went to sea
My mum and friends and don't forget me.
I ate the sandwiches I had to eat
Then took my socks off and paddled my feet
Then we came to Whitby swing bridge
Where we saw some waves forming a ridge.
As we passed it I saw Abbey ruins, standing tall
Surrounded by an old stone wall.
We stopped the boat to have some food,
We walked up a cobbled street
And had some fish and chips to eat.
After we had finished we put our rubbish in a bin
Licked our lips and wiped our chin.
We went back down to the boat
Where I put on my fleecy coat.
As the beautiful sunset sent rays of colour onto the sea,
We knew it was time to go home, Mum, my friends and me.

*Elizabeth Marsay  (8)*

## IRENE

Irene, vision and light,
Guidance and healing alike,
Teaching and giving,
O divine light,
Grounding and sounding out all that is right.
Living life often with a heavy load,
But always there for the divine folk,
Coaxing and scolding,
She brings us all on,
Teaching us all right from wrong.
Look inside, you say, we obey,
And what wonderful rainbows there we find.
I'm glad you are my friend and mentor,
For without you I wouldn't have a centre.

*Catherine M Simpson*

## WORD WAR TWO

*Bang!*
The bombs fall,
People buried, their terrified calls.
Taking shelter in the underground,
Every night when the warning sounds,
Wondering if your house will stand
After bombing from the Nazi lands.
Buildings destroyed, lives torn up,
Searching for possessions without much luck.
Musty, rubbery masks smothering your face,
Thick, choking smoke hanging over the place.
Silence in the shelters
*Bang!*
Is it us?
Trying to be cheerful throughout the fear,
War dragging on year after year.
Community spirit, working together,
Hope for peace, lasting forever.

***Laura Thompson  (10)***

## WHAT I SAW

Her naked child sat on the roadside,
Begging for nothing.

And all she has is there before you,
But all she has she gives to her child.

Day after day, hate, poverty and rejection,
That is all they know.

Only there's nothing I can do.
So how do I live, knowing that?

How do you live, knowing that?
And is there anything you want to do?

*Lizzie Cooper  (13)*

## SITWELL STEIN I WISH

At last, at last, the holiday we'd saved so hard to have
the train on time, then tube to where the plane was there
and so we flew away.
Landed, bussed and dropped at luxury hotel
nice room, clean sheets, to bed to sleep at last.

Morning. Sunny, sunny sun, jump out of bed,
'Hurray,' we said, 'breakfast on the balcony.'
The view was great, far distant hills then sea
but just below our pool, our blue, blue pool
and all around were sun beds.

Shiny, slimy, sun-oiled bodies loaded with towels and books
arrived at pool, oh, unwritten rule
'Ve are all reserved,' a sun bed said, 'zeeze towels tell you so.'
The Germans, the Germans are here.
Who said that life is a beach? Well, we'll fight for our pitch.

But not today. Today instead, a tour of town
buy postcards, take photos, look around.
Eat, drink and plan and plan and plan.

Earlier, earlier each morning earlier yet always too late
the Germans have been - completely unseen
and unwillingly sealed their fate.

The last day dawned, pale and wan
we wondered where the holiday had gone.
The plane was late, we sat and sat, then ate.
Parted for a shopping spree, something for him, tea for me.
He handed me a telescope, I handed him a bar of soap.

The flight was called, we boarded and sat
then he began to laugh and laugh.
'What have you done?' I said with dread

'Nailed a kipper under every sun bed,
the heat from sun and German bottom
very soon will send them rotten
and the smell will tell them where to go.'

*Pauline Smithson*

# LILLA CROSS

You stand alone upon the moor, the heather at your feet,
Around your head the breezes blow, the air is pure and sweet.
Through sun and heat and snow and gales, when loud the blizzards roar,
You've stood for thirteen hundred years and will for many more.
Out here where grouse and plover call, the folk who seek you find
A very ancient Saxon cross, the oldest of its kind.
And has it changed in all the years, this land of teal and snipe,
Where roe deer pass like fleeting ghosts, and meadow pipits pipe?
We know not, but through mists of time one tale has come down clear,
King Edwin of Northumbria ordered your presence here –
The first of England's Christian kings, his rule was firm and just,
But still he had his enemies, as even good men must.
A stranger came into the court, beneath his cloak, a sword.
He spoke fair words, 'I've come from far to greet my sovereign lord.'
The gate swung wide, he entered in, they hailed him as a friend,
He drew his sword, for Edwin then it must have been the end.
Not so - for swift as lightning flash across a darkening sky,
The faithful Lilla hurled himself, to save his king - and die.
Edwin, in grief and gratitude, vowed he would surely make
A tribute to this loyal soul, who perished for his sake.
And so you stand there, Lilla Cross, through rain and wind and storm,
A stone memorial to a man whose heart was brave and warm,
Reminding us, in this our age of greed and cowardice,
Of man's best gift to brother man, supreme self-sacrifice.

*M Urquhart*

## ANCIENT AND MODERN

The church clock tolls,
The hour marked, time moves on.
Across the churchyard, quiet in death
A silent sentinel stands tall
And comments not upon the labours lost
To that, whose chimes still beckon all
To brave the sharp October winds.
No malice, no grudge it bears,
Because no more its walls do ring
To the sweet chant of eventide;
Or because, where once the gloried
Coloured glass hid all,
One can now peep toward a ruined space,
A pillar'd hall in whose once
Sheltered, cloistered embrace,
Generations stood and pray'd,
Like those today,
Across the churchyard, quiet in death,
Amongst the oaken pews
Of St Thomas new, at Heptonstall.

*Alan Whitworth*

## SILENT BATTLE

Old Wrench wants to build in our garden -
An extension, he says, for his shop.
Our trees and his ivy will perish.
And the rats? They'll just move on elsewhere.

The council have granted permission
Since he plied them with chickens and steaks.
He shrugs at our 'provincial' objections:
'You can always move on elsewhere.'

Why waste our efforts in protest?
In silence we've plotted and planned.
Our weapons are hid in his ivy -
So we won't be moving elsewhere.

Dawn-break brings hard hats and diggers;
In the mire, they're forced to retreat.
For bats have built roosts in his ivy -
Well, he can always build it elsewhere . . .

***Beth Lomas***

## LADY IN WAITING

After spending all these months getting a lot bigger
Feeling tired and emotional and ruining your figure
They rush you into hospital saying, 'The moment has arrived,'
You thought pregnancy was bad enough and that you have survived

But this I hear you say, being prodded and in pain
No one seems to care, do the doctors have no shame?
Your modesty went out the door, all you want to do is shout
I want to get this over with, just get this baby out.

And Dad, what did he do? Well first he had the pleasure
Then he just sat back through nine months of leisure.
Yeah! He rushed you into hospital and carried in your case
He held your hand and chattered, whilst the sweat ran down your face.

Ah, and then that special moment, when the pain is washed away
With this little bundle in your arms you look down and say,
'You gave me hell, you made me cry, you caused me so much pain,
But you are just so wonderful I'd do it all again.'

There will be lots of laughter, tantrums and many tears
But this is just the beginning of many precious years.

*Lesley Ann Ball*

## DRIFTING

Drifting
Off to sleep,
Voices vanish.

Drifting
In your dreams,
Free and easy.

Drifting
On a cloud,
Weightless, timeless.

Drifting
To that place,
Problem solving.

Drifting
Light as air,
Stories merging.

Drifting
Round and round,
Where to settle?

Drifting
On and on,
Where's it ending?

Drifting
Drifting down,
Nearly there now.

Drifting
Touching earth,
Dreams are over.

Voices
Can be heard,
No more drifting.

*Angela Pritchard*

## WORLD OF CHEESE

Descended into a world of cheese
Where everything's so fake and phoney
All everyone wants to do is please
Because they're scared of being lonely
Yet every night they sit alone
And sob into their glass of wine
The Chardonnay tastes of bitter dreams
They crawl to bed at half-past nine
Then get up next morning
And paint on a smile
And laugh and pretend
But all the while
They just feel so empty
In this world of cheese where they have plenty.

*Caroline Crowther*

## 500 Miles

500 miles
It's what?
500 miles
It's not!
It is y'know
And takes twelve hours
All but a bit
Whichever way
You look at it
It's 500 miles.

Just a tick
A what?
A tick
A second spans
500 miles in thought
It's all that stands
'Twixt we and thee
It's just a tick
Well, maybe three.

You're what?
Alone?
You couldn't be
For we're your own
You're family
You're one of us
And life will prove.

There's just one thing
'Twixt thee and we
That's love
500 miles?
It's not.

*Paul Bracken*

## KEYS

Beware the man who carries keys
By way of his profession.
The more the locks, the more the keys,
The greater his discretion.

Beware the man who carries keys,
He takes due note of all he sees;
Tight mouth, a narrow, watchful eye,
He'll apprehend you by and by.

He does not scent the new-mown grass,
Or see the seasons as they pass;
His masters promise, soothe and prate,
But the man with keys stands at the gate.

*Colin Williamson*

## MORNING WALK TO WHITBY

Along the riverbank, the mist clings on,
Brought from the sea with last night's tide,
Reluctant to leave the safety of calmer waters.

Frost shimmers on the grasses and stones
Where early rays catch hold
Before it vanishes into darker shades of moisture.

The viewpoint from the empty viaduct
Overlooks us as we pass below,
A slight breeze gives warning of future blasts.

Here the dark, dank mud reveals treasures
For migrants and local residents alike,
Kittiwakes, oyster-catchers and elusive redshanks.

We pass the moored cobbles and smacks,
Perches for cormorants, sharp of eye and beak,
Awaiting the next tide's bounty.

Beneath the modern grey pillars ahead
We catch sight of the ochred Abbey ruins,
Whitby town beneath,
Our walk completed.

*Gillian Orton*

## Seasons

Sad it seems when petals fall off.
The tulip king's crown is lost.

The shine of summer drowns the spring,
The young girl's lost to the woman within.

The summer flowers' petals have formed.
The beautiful woman, voluptuous and tall.

The autumn comes, the flower is done, its leaves are golden and cold.
The woman has matured, middle-aged and bold
Her family has grown like the summer she used to know.

The winter arrives, the woman has withered with life.
The flowers have died.

The seasons of life will take all of time.

*Kimberley Jenkinson*

## FORGOTTEN LAND

Roof timbers bent with age
Wearily rest on granite walls
Doors and windows flap in the wind
Eventually falling to the ground

Inside a past life can be seen
Wood and stone, a rusting stove
A view of the fields now overgrown
No more spring crops to be sown

Creaking farm tools rattle and whine
Collapsing with the passage of time
Skeletal crows hang from a fence
Bounty paid in shillings and pence

Spoonhill Wood mysteriously sits
Its secrets wrapped in weeds and vines
Big old oak trees still enchant
While watching over its habitants

Farmyard animal sounds no more
Cobbles grace the courtyard floor
The pigsty smells a little sweeter
The cesspool dry and full of creeper

Weary bodies laid to rest
No one willing to take the task
The hustle of a working farm
Gently succumbing to peaceful calm

*John Mutton*

## ONE NIGHT IN PENNYWELL

The sound of broken glass shatters the still night,
loud music from a ghetto-blaster out of sight,
children stir in their beds and cry with fright.

Drunken yobs shout outside the door,
jagged glass lies on the floor,
please oh God, no more, no more.

Police cars screeching up the street,
then the sound of running feet,
no more music, no more beat.

When all is quiet and they've all left,
I actually feel a little bereft,
I can't even say it was a theft.

Just some kids out drunk and bored,
drinking alcohol they can ill afford,
doing things that can't be ignored.

I hope tonight things remain tranquil,
and there's no more need for the Bill,
or I will be needing more than a pill.

*Julie Long*

## FAR BEYOND FEY WEATHERHEATH

Far beyond fey Weatherheath
Where many fear to tread,
'Tis said in tale and song aplenty,
A river did then wind.
But no mere body of water,
Was that which ran so cold,
For ever of this detailed place,
But fell tales now are told.
Yet how wondrous a thing,
For great were flow and pureness,
Of the water silver,
Sun-adorned with gold.
Yet bleak and cold
Were its surrounds,
And dread did ever linger.
And how greatly then afeared,
Were all who saw its coils,
For in its very self it was
Evil given life.
And now the mortal sands
Are cold and grey indeed,
For none shall ever venture there,
To warm that place of searing unlove,
Whose very hands are ice.
Yet not ever was this so,
For in happy times is it said,
That folk aplenty lived once there.
Yet gone are days so fair.

*Alexander David Graham*

# THE NEW PIT BATHS

Naked miner admires new pit bath
with silver painted lockers
all numbered in ebony black
that glisten under neon lights.

Shower sprinklers await baptism,
and blackened body strolls onward
clutching mottled soap and pristine towel.
Expectation is now at fever pitch.

Gleaming, daunting plumbing awaits
and with dexterous ease, water cascades.
He languishes for heavenly minutes
as heat permeates his tired body.

Unsullied, refreshed, he dries lithe
body with enthusiastic zeal
and a bracing tingle engulfs his body
as he dresses at his leisure.

Now he's ready for the world
as his tuneless whistle reverberates
around the piercing pit yard.
Homeward he saunters for a well-earned rest.

***Alex Branthwaite***

## LIFE'S CYCLE

Dandelions, daisies, given free reign
Eddy and sway playing a graceful game
Lawn immaculate, now a foot high carpet
Creating for insects a dew-strewn banquet
Cherry blossom petals a floating regatta
Old roses droop, heady with attar
Soft fruits luscious trailing rampant and wild
Sunflower towers high with stubborn pride
Jasmine tiptoeing up walls meek and mild
Risks choking by zealous ivy beguiled
A child's paradise loved and respected
Evolving jungle so unexpected
Escaping the snip-snap of pruning shears
Symptom of owners' declining years
Through scented leaves of memories she sighs
Hoping strong hands will treasure what lies
Glory hidden 'neath unruly disguise
Returning to nature, ignored by man
Life's cycle all part of greater plan
Her soul - God's butterfly, its wings beating
To rhythm of celestial greeting.

*Kathleen Potter*

# DEAR FRIEND

Dear Jesus, may I speak with You
Share some private thoughts
A word or two?
Sometimes we all feel ill at ease
Mixed emotions hard to appease.
Feel so down, so alone
No one to take one's hand
Or share one's plans.
I am Your lenient servant
Your wish is my command
Lead me day by day
In this greatly troubled land.

*Mary Veronica Ciarella Murray*

## VALENTINE'S DAY

This day to lovers is dedicated
With no exceptions of any kind,
Therefore we are also included,
For are we not of one mind?

A day for tender communion,
And gazing in one another's eyes,
For travelling in one direction
Well mostly, though sometimes otherwise.

This is a day, no matter how few
Or many have massed up behind,
In fact the more the better; that's true
Of most men, and all woman-kind.

A day for Eve and Adam-ing
New Eden balanced yearly between
Bleak winter cold and first blossoming,
Leaf fall, and leafage once more green.

May lovers a new equilibrium embrace
At least as pilgrims following their star;
And also stood happily face to face
Perfected in all they do and are.

*Alan C Brown*

## FLOWERS IN SPRING

They show their fresh faces amid the new green;
their tiny white heads are a joy to be seen:
while trumpeting yellow spreads permanent sun,
defiant of snow, hail and rain, they have won.
The beads of the morning adorn them like pearls
as they proudly prevail over sallies and swirls,
for March winds are harsh and would do our friends harm;
yet, despite this onslaught, the blooms hold their charm.
Their beauty transcends all that nature may throw:
the gale and the hailstorms, the rain and the snow,
for their vision remains both in mind and in view
to enhance our enjoyment, our lives to renew
once again: every year, they create that effect;
every year they demand, and command, our respect.
As long as these snowdrops besprinkle our days,
as long as these daffodils lighten our ways,
and bluebells and hyacinths and crocuses spring forth
we've fair compensation for winds from the north.
So what if the elements attempt to spread gloom?
They fail in the face of spring Britain in bloom.

*Adrian Brett*

## MEANT TO BE

Without you I was nothing
All joy, all aspiration gone
No hope survived, no future
Had our love run its course?
I feared I'd lost your heart forever
Never more to see your smile
It was not lost, just interrupted
Gone missing, for a while
A smouldering within your heart
Now ignited has conceived
A flame to burn forever
A resurrection of our life, our love
A phoenix born of our distress
I'll love you more, because of it
Repay you all my days
Let's love away our troubles
Let passion free our soul
We are one, we are connected
We were meant to be.

*John Robinson*

## IMMOBILE

Imagine my embarrassment,
I have no mobile phone.
Everybody's got one,
To prove they're never really alone.
No matter where you go,
All you can hear is bleep, bleep, bleep,
I even hear it in my dreams,
When all I want to do is sleep.
In the car you'll see them,
One hand on the wheel as they yackity-yack.
It beats me how they don't have an accident,
Or keep the car on track.
Still I suppose there's one saving grace
Of these mobiles of yours,
It's the only time a man is ever likely to say,
'Mine is smaller than yours.'

*George Carrick*

# PICNIC CHECKLIST

The thermos is filled
With sweet lemonade
The pâté seems luscious
With port, it was made

Brie, grapes and baguette
Not much left to cook
Paper, pen ready
To write more of my book

Mozart is waiting
To be played while we sit
The blanket's tucked in
Our lantern will be lit

The chowder is finished
The basket is packed
I'm ready to go fetch
My flowered straw hat

The muffins look tasty
The salads are crisp
Now all I need is
Your warm summer's kiss.

*Marie A Golan*

# DOWN AT QUARRY BANK MILL

Airplanes repeat circles overhead
Taxis race frantic to Terminal 1 or 3
Peace reigns in the adjacent rural idyll
It's quiet at the dark, satanic mill you see

Yet two hundred years ago we heard
Looms and mules creating their din
Men, women and children sweat and toil
Producing the cotton to spin

The water wheel keenly turning
Converting the river into clout
To power all the frenzied activity
That took place day in and day out

Apprentice children working hard
No escape from this twelve hour day
Cleaning and crawling beneath the looms
Punishment if you tried to run away

Is this what Blake had seen and heard
In our green and pleasant land?
Where money and power forsake all others
To give the mill owner a winning hand

And now all is still and the birds sing
A far cry from those dark days
Yet, there is still so much more to learn
Of our past and our ancestors' ways.

*Nikky Braithwaite*

## My Manchester

So it always rains in Manchester? A fallacy! Not true!
The clouds are cold reminders of events like Peterloo,
Soul destroying workhouses too evil to be true,
Young urchins begging in the street, or bombs out of the blue.
Our city rose above this like the phoenix of the past,
And now we are creating a city made to last.
The Arndale Centre's re-emerged so folk can shop at leisure
And the Metrolink is there for each commuter's pleasure.
The Velodrome, and swimming pool have also made their mark,
And where the colliery once was, a new athletics park.
And when the Commonwealth event was opened by the Queen,
Mancunians were filled with pride (no dry eye to be seen).
Commonwealth athletes arrived to take part in the games,
And my, weren't we delighted to see such famous names!
Now we've reached the Lord's year of two thousand and four,
Manchester's not finished yet we've got to do much more,
And at the city's heart in Piccadilly Place,
Soon the world will marvel at the brand new civic space.
For what Mancunians do today the world will do tomorrow.
And as we're such a friendly lot, our ideas you may borrow.

*Margaret Doherty*

## CONTEMPORARY FOSSILS

Arcs of pebbles
like stretch marks across the damp beach.

They are cold to the touch.
And some sweat sea froth
like the infuriating paradox
of infantile fevers.

These anonymous little randoms,
are black and grey monotone
embryos.

Tightly drawn in kernels,
something like kidney beans.

They are the dead fossils
of barely developed
proto-children,

of ideas and idealistic plans,
of poems, and expressions of love,

flung onto shore
and crunched under the feet
of weekend walkers, walking.

Walking.

*Lee Simpson*

## LOOKING

Do you walk a lonely path
With an emptiness deep inside?
Are you looking for a real love
But does it always seem to hide?
No matter where you look
It's like the sun never shines and
All that's left is your darkness and
Your longing still to find.

*P Allinson*

## THE GREEN ROOM

I go there sometimes,
in meditation.
There are avocado tiles
on the floor
and dark green paint
on every door.
Along each wall ivy,
in variegated shades,
climbs and clings.

Alone, in a corner,
a stranger plays
a green piano and sings
to me while I bathe
in an aqua pool and
I listen to his voice,
soothingly cool.
The ceiling is made of
ice-green glass;
outside there are lawns
with uncut grass.
But here, I am safe from the
world outside.
Here I will hide,
in my haven.
My green room.

*Sara Newby*

## IT'S FUNNY HOW

It's funny how much I miss him now that he is gone,
It probably sounds stupid because he hasn't been gone for that long.
You could always tell when he was near,
I wish he was still here.

I remember when I used to go round
Every Sunday morning,
And Nana used to say, 'Go and wake him up.'
And I used to smile while he was busy yawning.

But then he became ill,
That's when the terrible day came,
My grandad became bedridden,
And couldn't play a single game.

He became very sick,
He didn't have the strength to smile,
And if he did get up,
It was only for a short while.

Then one dreadful day he died,
I refused to grieve,
For he was in pain no more
And was probably happy with the memories he did leave!

*Jessica Copland*

## THE LISTENER

Men in black jackets, the retiring room.
Conversations, 'politics, foreign affairs'.
Mahogany tables and leather-backed chairs.
Voices of wisdom, prophesising doom.
Clouds of smoke form silhouettes in the air.
Glasses overflowing, frothy beer and light ale.
Conversations, 'stocks, bonds and shares', fail
To impress the listener, pretending to care.

Men in flat caps, the working man's room.
Conversations, 'coal seams, who drew the short straw'.
Bar stools and tables chipped, beer stains the floor.
Voices heroic, tell tales of near doom.
Clouds of smoke form silhouettes in the air.
Glasses overflowing, frothy beer and light ale.
Conversations, 'tomorrow will be a brighter day', fail
To impress the listener, pretending to care.

Men in black jackets, men in flat caps, the listener observes.
Conversations of men, impassively she dispenses the beer.
Pretty as a picture, she will shed no tears.
Voices of men, 'Listen but don't be heard, it is your job to serve'.
Empty ashtrays as clouds of smoke form silhouettes in the air.
Collect pint glasses once overflowing with frothy bear and light ale.
Conversations she can take no part in, fail
To impress the listener, she does not care.

*Rachel Lucinda Burns*

# MY CAT

She came in late at night
I heard her footsteps,
Gentle and light,
I heard her whimper and whine,
The cry of the night, yet so divine,
Upon her toes, she gladly does dance
Like a cat in a mad trance.
I reach out to her, and she softly purrs,
Over and out, cat wants to be out.
Out in the hall, I do call, she leaps and bounds,
Her feet hardly touching the ground,
As I quickly unlock the door,
She dashes past outwardly bound,
Into the night, she starts screeching,
To her delight and I retire to my bed
And lay my head, to sleep
And hope, tomorrow my cat will come home.

*Jennie Stott*

# HABBANIYA SHADOWS

No goodbyes between swift magpies
Long tails wild doubled in flight
Look beyond, tree branches bend
First love awake will never end.

Watching days remember the view
Still lonely really, changes must
Spreading wings too swift, too far
Crystal tears reluctant to rust.

So to my dreams take heed
Ever sweet angel, lasting sighs
Opening passions chatter magpie blues
Covet my lips under star-kissed skies.

*Elsie Scrowther*

## SHE IS HERE

French lavender still lingers in the air,
announcing her presence as if she were there.
The room still warms with the essence of her,
a potpourri of emotions ready to stir.
Her empty bed holds onto reflections,
Wrapped in her aroma, tears, and affections.
Her dreams once played across these pillows of down,
sweet dreams of dancing in her emerald gown.
The room, undisturbed, since the day of her death,
is crammed with her being and the love of her breath.
She is the smile in the mirror, the waltz of the dust,
the shadow in the window, and the hair in the brush.
The very air whispers the sound of her laughter,
like an echo of her soul to remind us long after.
Intense love is tangible here in her empty domain,
but we carry her within us - an eternal flame.
Oh, how I yearn for the circle of her arms,
for those gentle kisses, like healing balms.
There were so many words I wanted to say,
so many days have been stolen away.
The sadness within, fills me with pain,
so I will visit her room to be with her again.

*June Macfarlane*

## BITTER SILENCE

The silence is worse than the long, drawn out scream
Of my frustrated mind filled with unfulfilled dreams,
For I no longer know what it is that I crave,
I am dying inside. Can I ever be saved?

There is something I want, that I desperately need,
To live out all the dreams that have long gone to seed,
But to conjure them up, to remember my aims,
Would bring pictures of hurt and of sorrow and pain.

So, resigned to a life of 'same s*** - different day'
I listen to time slowly ticking away,
If I'd taken the risk, pushed the hard times aside,
There wouldn't be silence, just pride and more pride.

*Claire Cockburn*

# IN LOVE AND PROUD

He's knocked my socks off
It feels like a dream
When I'm not with him
I just want to scream
He's blown my mind
I feel so secure
When he says my name
I know we're for sure
I'm all of a flutter
I'm all in a daze
Once we've made love
I want him again
I know I love him
I'm sure I do
A love like ours
Will always stay true
Just so long as he knows
Our love cannot die
As long as we're honest
And don't tell a lie
So listen to me
I'm talking with pride
*I am in love*
And I don't need to hide.

**Victoria A Miller**

# MILITARY MISERY

I often wonder as I steer my way
Along Northumberland's attractive lanes
How must these mountains, rivers, dales and plains,
Delightful to my eyes, have seemed the day
A band of soldiers found their passage barred
By Tyne's swift waters. Roman marching men,
Footsore and weary, seeking once again
A crossing place, an easy one to guard
Against the fierce Northumbrians of old,
Who fought from what's now Hexham, Corbridge, Wall,
A wilderness of green, a muddy sprawl
On rain-soaked slopes, and 'often bloody cold',
They'd grouse - in *Latin* slang, of course:
There were no bikes, so they'd say: 'On your horse'.

*Frank Littlewood*

## ROAD OF FRIENDSHIP

Silently I sit and wonder
Where my life will lead.
Which road do I turn down?
Will I have the things I need?

Will my friends be by my side
Or will I be alone?
Will I find a place I love,
A place I call my home?

Life is one long journey,
No one knows where it will end.
But I will have to take my chance
And hope you'll be my friend.

I hope you will be there for me
And I'll be there for you.
I pray each night I will awake
And know our friendship's true.

*Jacqueline Bolt  (16)*

# AWAKE

As the mind was tranquil in the refuge of dreams
Paroxysms of light stabbed its armour of sleep
Fluttering eyelids struggled to ease into the reality of the present,
A present not long ago entombed in the past.
Feelings evading the enticing grasp of memory
Rising from the abyss only to fall back again
Dark garments of time flung away, copper redness floating in,
The urge of dawn too faint, enveloped by a mist of nothingness
Pushing away the pall of oblivion
Silence eloquent in its admonition of the inactivity
The conscious subjected to visions unseen, cries unheard,
Sanity battling against the deluge of delusions
The myriad facets of life flash past,
Too quick for the languid mind, too slow to escape the tangles
                                        of the intellect
Free from one world, a prisoner in another!

*Rajiv Sankaranarayanan*

## MY SECRET PLACE

Sometimes although surrounded by noise and people
I am all alone.
Enclosed in my own quiet world wherein none can enter
Unless I wish it.
I can be sad or happy letting nobody disturb my peace,
My thoughts I control.
Once again I can talk and laugh with friends I've known
Thinking of what we did and said, though many are now dead.
Yet, they are alive in my mind.
Reality of life is hell, I can escape from it
By entering the separate world inside my brain.
Without this secret place of mine,
I would go insane.

*Dave Sim*

## CIRENCESTER ABBEY

Nothing is left.

> Only its shapes set down
> In concrete stepping stones
> In grass. And school groups
> Follow-their-leaders round

Its once-walled air.

> We trace the arc which bore
> A window, tangents where
> The brothers sang, the chords
> Which were a shrine, and now are

Emptied space.

> We picture it. We find
> The sky fan-vaulted, place
> The tower's highest point,
> Level bells with winds

Above the trees.

> We see that kites may pass
> Through stone, and jackdaws tease
> The sainted martyrs pierced
> By light alone. We look at

Absence there,

> But will not see it wholly,
> Cannot find that hair-
> Line crack that splits the air
> Open to where only

Nothing is left.

*Ann Heath*

## ANGER

I feel it pulsing through my veins
But never letting go of its reins
I feel it throbbing in my head
Making my body feel like lead
Don't want it to erupt
It would be like hot burning lava
Don't want to be abrupt
I really wouldn't rather
I want to be calm
But the thing won't go away
Don't want to cause harm
For it to come out to play
I want this anger to melt
I want it to go away

*Angela C Oldroyd*

## To Mum

She was the most beautiful woman in the world,
Good looking, a lovely figure, ever so clever, ever so wise.
She was a mum - a good listener,
A good sympathiser,
A very good disciplinarian,
One good telling-off was usually enough.

She was a wonderful cook,
Her sticky toffee pudding and jam roly-poly were delicious.
Oh and she made lovely Yorkshire puddings and delicious gravy.
I will never forget Mum; I still miss her.
I hope forever that she will watch over me.

*Janet Cavill*

# A SPRING POEM

Winter's cold grasp loosens slowly in a new season's warmth,
Primrose in elfin shyness, flirting with a gentle breeze
Under protective hedgerows, colours glowing in leafy shade,
Announce their presence to all.

A dawn chorus starts in hesitant song,
A hymn slowly rising to fill the air with sweet surprise,
Skylarks in full voice soar into the sky,
Duelling in the bright morning sun,
Silver chains of music cascading down in high, clear song,
To touch the heart with joy.

Feathered songsters plain and adorned,
Build their homes for new life as yet unborn,
Cocooned in their own small world,
Awaiting the miracle of birth.

Gentle breezes sighing through the trees,
Grass a verdant green,
Shielding in den and burrow,
The young of hunter and hunted in ignorance of a life yet to be,
Seeking only food and warmth, from vixen to doe.

This then is the miracle of life renewing,
The sight, scent, and sound of spring.

*M Cook*

## MY WAVERTREE

I take a walk down Sandown Lane -
It's a little cloudy, a chance of rain
'Morning Bill, how have you been?
Your front lawn's looking lush and green.'
I take a stroll into the park
And watch the dogs play and bark.
'Hello Buttons, you good boy -
Of course I'll throw your favourite toy.'
'Good day Mike - you feeling fine?
A little heady from last night's wine?'
I'll nip off home for tea and toast,
But first I'll mail some urgent post
At the pillarbox on the corner,
It feels as if it's getting warmer.
'All right Norm, it's looking up -
Fancy a quick one down the pub?'
Past the cricket field, the crack of wood,
He hits for six - by Jove he's good!
I push the door of the public house
And there stands Fred, quiet as a mouse;
A glitter shirt and a toothy grin,
I think he might have hit the gin!
Back home now to 95,
Workers' cars slowly drive . . .
Over policemen on the road
And safely to their own abodes.

*Jack Gray*

## SNAPSHOT

Painterly landscapes photographed,
bright clear light reveals beauty,
sunlight paints tiger stripes,
dazzling colour and deafening silence.

From a distant epoch ancient air is released
- a universal aesthetic.
Arched and muddied torrents,
collecting like beads of mercury on a huge horizon.

Pampering is not enough,
the claustrophobia sets in,
like being buried alive.

I'm old enough
                    to remember achieving the perfect death.

*Sheila Anderson*

## THE ESSENCE OF NATURE

Somewhere in the deep mystery of autumn,
an answer to 'what does it mean?'
lies where colours creep with time,
in leaves leaving sycamore green;
the morning skies bear glorious gold,
comes a breeze to trick our ear.
residents of the eaves are
only an avian memory near.
A pastel rose of beauty fades,
petals to the cooling ground,
the evening dew is born
now shimmering, commonly found,
brooding clouds of grey,
shield a reluctant sun,
into sleep the dormouse slips
the stream is quicker to run.

Why this sense of departure . . .
indeed this sense of hello . . .
the bestowal of amber and bronze . . .
but a bee that has to go?
Is it a purpose brought
the passing of what must be?
Surely it's the essence of nature,
the grace of God, given to see.

*Andrew Gruberski*

# RESPECT

God be in the universe,
In the clouds, as they drift by.
God be in the stars at night,
And in the moonlit sky.

God be in the mountains,
God be in the trees,
God be in the very earth,
God be in the seas.

God be in the wondrous flowers
And in the butterflies.
God be anywhere at all,
But God be in my eyes,

So everything I ever see,
Every sound I hear,
Every human hand I touch,
Each heart that I hold dear,

I will respect with all the love
You show unconditionally,
To very single one of us.
Dear God, please be in me.

*Lorna Lea*

## HOLDERNESS SPRING

Now garden paths
are dressed in pink
frail blobs of blossom
torn from trees
by yesterday's rain.

Today blackbirds again
patrol the lawn
casting cautious eye,

and on the broken fence
two doves sing and look
as if they're loving spring.

*Graham Wade*

# TIME

Each one gone . . . a memory
of love and laughter and tasks
well done,
of courage, ambition,
achievements won.

Failure, sadness, fear and sorrow
don't dwell upon.
Strive for fulfilment in those
to come.

Precious assets for us to use,
to prize, to savour.
To sow, to harvest - no waste
in kind.
There are no seconds
of the seconds of time.

***Margaret Dennison***

## SPRING

Sunlight through the trees, lighting the forest, dark,
Each brilliant strip of light, accentuating the bark,
Trees casting their shadows, some long, others short,
Hiding in the darkness, woodland creatures caught.
Snowdrops fading as crocuses, stretch up for the light.
Daffodils sprouting quickly, give brilliant yellow sight.
The earth is warming slowly, little buds begin to burst,
Giving forth their flowers, all wanting to be first.
Many varied colours, outside of winter's back door,
Make the world much brighter. Spring is here, once more,
Birds chirruping in the treetops, a chorus to the dawn,
Glad that day to be alive, happy they were born.
People start to see and hear, all of spring's delights
Glad at last to be free, of winter's cold dark nights.

*Roy Hare*

# COLOUR OF WATER

No colour, they say of water,
But that is just not true at all
As it takes on many colours,
Whether it's rill or waterfall.

The sea can be a sunny blue;
A river can be brown or grey;
A shady cove be emerald green,
As it all depends on the day.

A brook can ripple with diamonds,
With sparkling sunshine in its hair;
While gold can dance among the waves,
Stay shimmering and golden fair.

A cavern's water, black as night,
From a cascading waterfall
Silver merrily, laughingly, falls,
Having a wonderful ball.

Pools may reflect fluffy white clouds;
Meres and streams take on many hues.
It all depends on wind or sky,
And even lakes can have the 'blues'.

*J Millington*

## LAVENDER BUSHES

The lavender bushes were dying.
Edging the pathway they
formed a perfumed walkway
to the house.
I used to brush my hands along them
as I ran.
The scent breaking free,
lifting my spirits
and filling my senses.
Aromatic memories
of childhood's summer days.
A sweet nectar
of laughter and tears,
love and caring,
happiness and innocence.
I think of you now
and the life we shared.
But the house lies empty.
Shuttered windows like closed eyes
and the lavender bushes
were dying.

*Anne Hamlett*

# FISH TOUR

Sometimes estuary fever brings exploring days;
We followed the Hull Fish Trail round various Old Town ways.
Exchange Court Alley led us to a curious cast iron squid;
And on Minerva Terrace we found at length a quid.
On Hull's 'sidewinder', *Arctic Corsair* (Cod War Veteran),
We learned about their hardships from an old-time trawler man.

Meanwhile, down the fish dock, 'mid boxes, foam and ice,
Dad hungers for his haddock, chips, tartar sauce and rice.

Alas! The supermarket showed no piscatorial glut;
Every fridge for fish had failed - electrics had gone phut!
And 'Fried Fish Fred' was shut all week - which left us in a stew.
Going home, Dad's gutted. Whatever shall we do?

Our Tunny solved the cuisine: 'Tomatoes, 'cumbers, greens!'
So while she set the table I de-canned seven sardines.

*Howard Peach*

## BLACK GOLD

The sound of the buzzer alerts the men
Time to get up for the day shift again
Cats in chorus with barking dogs
Miners walking in sparking clogs
Secured in the cage and down they go
Into the bowels of the earth below
Crawling on their bellies into pitch-black hell
Chipping black gold out of seams to sell
Risking their lives just to earn a crust
Short of breath with lungs full of dust
Sons followed fathers down the pit shaft
When conditions improved; it was still hard graft
Women were the backbone of the home
Up at dawn to get work done
Copper in the kitchen came to the boil
Washing day started with sweat and toil
With carbolic soap they rubbed and scrubbed
On a board that was fastened over the tub
Coal fire oven to cook our food
Home-made bread to fill her brood
Porridge for breakfast and broth for tea
Good hearty meals for the family
When the buzzer silenced on that sad day
The end of an era came our way
No future prospect in mining coal
Men on the scrap heap collecting dole
Community spirit is what we had
In our mining village when I was a lad.

*Carol Kaye*

## MY CITY AND I
*(Main course)*

The view comes with the office lunch, a well chewed
slab of damp Bradford. I start with a grey-green
ridge where Peel Park (or is it the cemetery?), ends
in trees, some with leaves in November still,
fringing a terrace that slopes by a road, dropping
down to meet one, busier, where the traffic
swirls like a moorland stream, and in a tuna
with salad on brown oven-bake, the phrase
turns up, babbling, 'My city and I.'
I try it again. The first person singular,
under flat caps, scarves, prayer hats and wind-blown
umbrellas, is at one with the entity
that's as busy as far as my eye can see.

Wiping my lips with Sandwich Express' napkin,
I think of love of place, and how it's served up
in hot-blooded contrasts: in crenellated
chimney pots playing hard to get, in that come-hither
finger of grey, by Broadgate. Once there was
a somewhere else, my Heaton, a parish pump
amourette, but I am over her now. And I reckon
I fancy 'it', that sexy pronoun, dressed
to the nines in distance and weather; and me
with this sixth sense that I'll be bedded out there.
Its spread-eagled intimacy is working
at me like a toothpick, easing that irksome
strand of tuna from between my teeth.

**Bruce Barnes**

# A Village Pond

Often the pond can be found at the end of the main street in the village.
After heavy storms the street is awash, and the pond takes the spillage.

There is a wooden bench, firmly fixed to a solid cement base.
Where pensioners sit and chat, age firmly etched on their face.

Children can be seen with nets and jam jars, fishing for the stickleback.
There are ducks with their heads underwater, who then sit up
and quack.

Winter comes, now the pond is frozen, and the ducks are trying to
keep their feet.
The villagers bring bread to the birds, when the snow covers the street.

The robin, blackbird, wren and sparrow, can be seen hopping about.
Spring is round the corner, the pond has thawed, now the ducks
can wade about.

Now spring is almost upon us, the pond's banks now have daffodils.
Primroses and king cups can be seen, and there is still snow on the hills.

Now the trees are in leaf, some with cherry blossom, in pale shades
of pink.
Now the winter is over, the pond is no longer like a skating rink.

It is now covered in lilies all floating alongside the bulrush.
Also the red roots of the willow tree, with tadpoles swimming in a rush.

Most villages have a pond, some small, some big, in their main street.
Most have ducks, some have swans, and some are shallow, some
very deep.

There is one village pond, of which I am very fond.
So when out for the day at Beverley, visit Walkington village pond.

*David Bielby*

## UNTOUCHED

As I sit and gaze and think of ways of opening and changing the
Eternal doors, I realise it is not possible, like the

Mist upon the moors. The wonderful sights to behold are free,
if only you would look and see, the beauty is all

Around, untouched by man's hands living in the ground. We take
for granted these precious gifts each and

Every day, the wonder of the rainbow and the Milky Way.

When we realise within our mind, we will eventually come in contact
and we will find the essence sublime.

Creativity is within our scope, we then will be in tune with the Divine.
We can only wish and hope, this to be

True, in the way we live like the morning dew.

Nature has a way of compensating in areas not seen, to bring forth the
knowledge with splendour to all

Human beings, the answers are already within our sight to understand
that love is always first and foremost,

Right.

*Matthew Wilson*

## THE WORD OF GOD

Some believe, some perhaps not
In something which they all know
Which will bring them joy and solitude
A goal which they can clearly show
That faith is made through confidence
In a Heavenly creed
A doctrine in which we must all assent
To a word we must all heed
The word of God is an honoris causa
In which we all must crave
To love our fellow man, woman and child
It's not too late before we join the grave
The masses now are growing fast
Belonging to one church, one following
A body eternal which will forever last.

*Leslie Bailey*

## CHAOS

Glimmering sunbeams dancing hand in hand
A serene rhythm flickering across your eyes
The contentment is reclaimed once more
Almost like it was never missed
Yet only too soon it gets wrenched away
The clouds sweep past
Blocking all the beams
Anger overwhelms as satanic voices take heed
A split second of solicitude until
This hellish society blacks out.

The flickering in your eyes is turned to an instinct of animosity
Hesitant features upon a frozen skin
An unspoken vow between the two
It echoes through the air, and rattles inside my skull
With slight indignation as a fist of wind blows
Leaving a motionless figure twisting and distorted
Dying on the ground beneath a multitude of violence

As the heart begins to bleed, emotions gush
Seeping through the skin
A miscellaneous sound of silence and screams
The fire within becoming a synthesis of feelings
Of a mind both ruthlessly torn apart by devotion
And in turmoil of revulsion towards the yellow-faced mist.

*Nadia Hashim*

## IN PASSING

Some time between the depths of night
and the break of day
love.
We murmur a profound truth
and the night light listens.

*Victoria Bonner*

## COLD TURKEY

Ranting, raving, displaying a desperate craving.
Begging, pleading
Wild-eyed
Sweaty-browed, he rocks and rolls
Brought low
Begging, pleading
Desperately needing
A habit so hard to feed
All-consuming, panic looming
Animal-eyed.

'C'mon doc be, pal' his entreaties we must resist
To help him desist.
He gasps, pants, still he rants, guts he spews
As his face changes hues.
His craving totally enslaving.
Sweat pours behind the doors.
His body a broken mess from pharmacological excess.
He sweats, he screams as in frightful dreams.
His mind cannot defend against, hobgoblins, foul fiends
Turning day to endless night.

Sweaty brow, breathing fast, rocking, rolling in stomach cramps
Desperate craving, raving, mind unhinged, cos he binged
On alcohol, heroin, methadone, 'whizz', crack
Anything he could find to help him unwind.
How he raves, rants, screams, in terrible dreams
An empty shell in a private hell
Begging, pleading, for release and peace.

*Maddoc Martin*

## ON SWIRL HOW

The mist played its dancing game,
for me to view and to pause,
at the lacy wisps,
blowing across the linking hause

Prison Band, a jagged rampart,
protecting an airy castle,
studded with ancient rocks,
like a crazily-built bastle

On a snaking path,
did Prison Band begrudgingly yield,
and a wonderful mountain became conquered,
from behind that splintered shield.

*Ken Parker*

## VISITING MY AUNT

Out to the yard at the dead of night, or
the white pot under the bed?

And always nights when the cold wind moans
and shadows move on the shed.

Torch and wellies, overcoat, of course the rain's
still falling.

Down the stairs and up the yard, the curse of
nature calling.

Bursts of moonlight, gusts of wind, that creaking
hinge on the door.

Walls with holes where spiders live, something
moves on the floor.

Ghouls and witches, owls and frogs, the fear of
little green men.

Could be almost anything when one is only
ten.

Throne like ice, old news for wipe, trust it were
no fun.

The thing was just to concentrate, to do the
deed and run.

But all of these are memories now, no more the
cold and rush.

A step or two and sit yer down, and afterwards
just flush.

*P Jennison*

## SPOILS OF WAR

Their bodies lie in caverns underground,
Where bombs once echoed there is no sound.

Peace, victorious, lies purple and bruised,
Tainted with bloodshed, torn and confused.
Earth's fields in hues of honour abused:
War, now triumphant, cannot be excused.

An institution of generations:
Annihilation of populations.

Who is the man who dares to mock
At gates of Hell I fear to knock?
What beast is this that roars with pride
Where love and truth have been denied?

In our grief or discontent
Remember that we weave peace yet,
Loves long lost we may lament
But celebrate lest we forget.

*E M Doyle*

# LADIES OF A CERTAIN AGE

Sitting in rows, grey puffball perms
Granny roses on billowing frocks, lisle
Stockings display purple worms
With age they have almost come to terms

Owl-rimmed specs under pencilled arches
Ginger or black
Too heavy as age marches on to the beat of
The Bowls Club, the Whist Drive and
Afternoon tea -
Wishing they could be free of the
Stockings and roses, the specs and the teeth
Whilst still feeling sixteen underneath.

Restriction of vests and hammock-size bras,
Big pink knickers
All covered with flowers, or under-slips
And fat padded hips
Painted claws and bright red lips.

Legs akimbo they sit and enjoy
Sucking nuts and breadless crusts
Breasts meeting belly,
Laughing and sleeping whilst watching the
Telly
Hoping for someone to call and agree
That they are special
And invite them for tea.

*Delyse Holmes*

## OUR MOTHER EARTH

Is there hope and glory here
On this Earth, we hold so dear?
Is this land our sacred ground
Where bones of ancestors are found?
Are the oceans, rich and deep
Forever ours to fish and keep?
What if waters, dry to sand
And trees fall, too weak to stand?
Will the sky, remain so blue?
Will man honour all that is true?
We need the sun, the moon and stars
We need these things, for these are ours
Time's lost forever, if we fail
To save our world, which is so frail.

Every song will tell a story
A story of pain, love and glory
Every book will tell about life
A history of suffering, greed and strife
Tales will be told of past and future
The knowledge of people of every culture
Times will change, just like the seasons
Bad things will happen, for no real reason
Wars and pollution will ravage our lands
And Earth may soon, turn into sand
Greed and ignorance, will be to blame
That is our legacy, and also our shame
How do we explain to our next generation
The catastrophe caused by our devastation?
Our land will die, and so will we
There will be no place, for us to flee.

*Gordon Greenfield*

## TRUE LOVE TRUTH

Abed I lie
And wonder why,
She left me here
Alone a'tear,
To fathom out
What love's about.

My child of three
She took to be
With her, and worse,
That boy of course.
Then left no word
Where to be heard.

So this New Year,
So full of cheer,
Reminds me that
The child who sat
Upon my lap
Has left this gap.

To love again
Is hard, for pain
Is what I see
Love, for to be.
It's pain you'll feel
When love is real.

*Ian Godfrey*

# WHAT HAVE YOU DONE FOR ME?

You came and changed our lives for the better.
We made adjustments for you.

We started to see good times with you beside us.
We were lucky to have a son like you.
We counted our blessings.
We adored you,
Rolling out the red carpet
Wherever you stepped.

Now you are big and ugly enough to look after yourself.
You asked us not once, but many times
'What have you done for me?'

You ask me, son!

Ask me about the twenty years I have spent on you.
I neglected my career and my own luxuries for you.
We gave you the best!

All our sacrifices may be worthless to you now

Ants ate away at me when I saw you in pain when you were small.
However, now you are eating away at me.

Remember son, one day your day shall come,
When your child shall ask you,
'What have you done for me?'

Start practising because we sure didn't!

*Parveen Saini*

## THE HOSPITAL VISIT

I looked in my diary and what did I see?
A hospital appointment for little old me.
I got up early not wanting to be late
I'd got to be ready for half-past eight
The ambulance men will be here once more
Soon they will be knocking on my door
Saying, 'Are you ready? It is a nice day.'
Then I get into the ambulance and go on my way
Up in a lift and into a waiting room there
Seated comfortably in my cosy wheelchair
After the doctors and nurses I see
I go back home as fit as can be.

*Laura Chaplin*

## THE SUMMER ROSE

Cooler breezes whisper
Now the skies are turning grey
Summer days are ending
Autumn's on its way

Whisper to the summer rose
To bow unto her fate
Silently the red rose sighs
She knows it is too late

The glory days are over
Her petals float to ground
Like velvet-cushioned teardrops
They fall without a sound

Whisper to the red rose
Cool breezes of the air
Return to us next summer
All is not despair.

*Shirley May Croxford*

## MERMAID

I want to be a mermaid
And flick my tail in the sea.
Sitting frozen on Filey beach
Is *not* where I want to be!

Mermaids are so romantic,
They frolic in clear blue water
With lithe bodies and pretty names -
Not known as 'Jessie's daughter'.

They swim along the shoreline
Of isles with silver sand.
*Their* mothers don't sit knitting
With newspapers close at hand.

I want to be a mermaid
And flick my tail in the sea.
Slumped here in damp cold sand
Is *not* where I long to be!

*Brenda Artingstall*

# ODE TO CHARLIE B

You came into our lives when you were only one,
just a little older than a pup!
With your ruby coat and soft brown eyes,
we couldn't believe our luck!
We told you your name was Charlie B
and you replied with a deep, but friendly bark!
Whatever the weather on your daily walk,
you were as happy as a lark!

Your favourite haunt was The Bluebell Woods,
where you met all your canine pals,
You were part of the woodland landscape
in all seasons of the year
and on weekend nights you gave the local pub
customers always some hearty cheer!
Poor old Tina, who is wheelchair-bound,
ever loved your comforting stare

Xmas Eve walks were such a joy,
how you loved all the bright festive trees with lights.
Now you're gone, will this year's Xmas walk,
somehow not seem right?
Charlie, you welcomed a kitten in your twilight years
and, being a sport, you gave little Monty no reason a dog to fear!
No problems as canine, feline friends,
for you both after silly arguments, made very warm amends!

When you turned almost fifteen years old,
you tried to fight being both ill and old,
but your end had sadly come, the vet us reluctantly told!
As you arrived at Canine Heaven's door,
lordly Mentor, he welcomed you.
The golden gate was opened and Charlie, you passed through!
There was no need for us this tragic day with endless tears to rue.
For when you passed into eternal sleep, Mentor had lit his
                                        candle for you!

*(Mentor - The Canine God)*

**Stephen J Bolton**

## BRIDLINGTON HEROES

When the tempest arose on that stark winter's day
The sea quickly swelled into mountainous waves.
There was danger to challenge in Bridlington Bay,
But Christopher Brown was a fisherman brave.

The sea quickly swelled into mountainous waves,
There were breakers which made the boldest man quail.
But Christopher Brown was a fisherman brave,
In rescuing wrecked sailors he wouldn't fail.

There were breakers which made the boldest man quail,
As Christopher was joined by harbour-side friends.
In rescuing wrecked sailors they couldn't fail
Though none of them knew how their dark night would end.

Christopher was joined by harbour-side friends,
Good Bridlington fishermen, sturdy and true.
Though none of them knew how their dark night would end,
They rescued the ailing Victoria's crew.

Good Bridlington fishermen, sturdy and true,
Challenged the danger in Bridlington Bay.
They rescued the ailing Victoria's crew
When the tempest arose on that stark winter's day.

*Mike Wilson*

## BRADFORD (WEST YORKSHIRE)

Bradford is a nation of its own
Where the Asians are well-known
For their curry houses and restaurants
If you have a vindaloo, you'll end up in the loo
Or if you have madras, you will end up with lots of gas

We have the Bradford Bulls
As well as Bradford City
Put them together and they're very pretty
Plus there is the Photography Museum
So why not come to see them?

The 'Pulse' is our local radio
And you can listen to them while on the 'go'
You can get a bus, or train
Or even, maybe, an aeroplane

We also have lots of other cuisine on the scene too,
Just waiting to be tried and seen by you.

*Coleen Bradshaw*

## FIRST MEETING

I saw you and my
Body groaned, ached.
The look that launched
The arrow.
And I, your unlikely
Target.
Bullseye!

You spoke to me
And I saw the
Redness of the inside
Of your mouth.
And I had to
Fight the overwhelming
Need to feel your bottom
Lip between mine,
To run my tongue against it.

Alcohol.
Courage.
The excuse to stand
So close to you.
Side by side,
But not daring to actually
Touch.
Music.
Movement, sway.
Your fingertips on the
Inside of my thigh.
I am alive!
Charged . . .

It took two hours
Until our lips met.
Four hours until
You got yourself
Inside me forever.

I don't even
Know you.
But I can't help
Loving you.
My insomniac eye
Dreams only of you.
But you do not
Dream of me.
You are gone.

*Rebecca Culpan*

# THE FERRYBOAT
*(Over to the Black Isle)*

Collected empty bottles to sell,
A few pennies I must have,
I want to go on the ferryboat,
Yes! Times were hard,
It was the nineteen-forties,
Ten years old I am,
'Come in for your tea,' my mother called,
'And wash your hands.'
'Ma! I want to go on the ferryboat,
Please! Please! Can I?'
'We will see what tomorrow brings,
Sit down and ask your da.'
'Take your tea with your brothers,'
My da said, 'and we will have a chat,
Have you all been good today?'
'Yes, we have.'
'I have saved a few bob,
A picnic on Saturday we will have.'
Yes! We will all go on the ferryboat,
Called the Eilean Dubh.

***Muriel Mabon***

## MUSIC MAN

In comes the Music Man
Each week at half-past five,
Lip flexibilities and tonguing
Will help the music come alive.
Learning scales,
Like hoisting sails,
Hunting for the note she missed;
Like hunting for whales in a thick sea mist.
Practising arpeggios
Up and down the music goes,
Raised a twelfth or sixteenth,
Reaching notes between gritted teeth.
The theory books give the lips a rest
But put her memory to the test.
Compound time or grouping notes,
Rests and ties or beaming,
Whatever the question she gets right
All fetch her smile up beaming.
On with the lesson
Whether waltz, samba or jive
Musician plays the best she can
Her heart in the music brings it alive.
In comes the Music Man
Each week at half-past five,
As he teaches and coaches
Musician really comes alive.
He leaves again at half-past six,
Complete with his bag of tricks,
Leaving behind a little of himself
And music no longer on a shelf.

*Dan Maughan*

## WHAT IS MINE IS YOURS

Alyson was praised for her drawing
the drawings she uses for design
which come out of my daily sketch book
of the people I meet every day

Alyson was a mediocre drawer
at school but friends she had
who needed someone to ghost
and trace she used even for Planet

Lucinda also used by the department
could at least draw, for Marks and Sparks
hang on, hadn't we all nearly died back home
for our Jewish brethren and here they don't care?

All our admiration and our bravery for so long
has ended up like this, for this island
our talent copied by the mediocre of this land
not even the best, to save a corrupt department.

And they used plenty more . . .
as royals turned a blind eye,
ours weren't so easily lied to
and we call it theft
telling them it was science
which scientists loudly refute . . .

***Renate Fekete***

## IT'S ONLY MONEY

Whatever happened to all that money?
Can't stop laughing, though it isn't funny.
Chipping away at an endless block,
Now it's all gone, it's a dreadful shock.
It was a delight to receive such a letter,
Suddenly everything seemed much better.
Lots of friends appeared on the scene,
All these years, where have they been?
Endless parties, having fun,
Exotic locations, days in the sun.
Expensive jewels for me to treasure,
Designer clothes, so much pleasure.
Fancy restaurants, what a great time,
But I just didn't know where to draw the line.
Now it's all over, and I'm sitting alone,
In my beautiful house, it's not a real home.
There ends my story, along with my cash,
I'm working again, so I really must dash.

*Susie Field*